THE STONES OF STRATHEARN

Andrew Finlayson

GU00984726

ONE
TREE
ISLAND
PUBLISHING

The many people and animals who assisted and encouraged this work are acknowledged on page 83 but I wish to note here how particularly grateful I am to the Society of Antiquaries of Scotland for permission to reproduce the many illustrations from their Proceedings noted 'PSAS' in the text.

Front cover top; Midwinter sunset Tullybannocher.
Front cover top line from left; Gleneagles stone A, Crofthead, Tullybannocher, Lawers, Dunruchan stone A, Dalchirla east stones.
Title page; Dunruchan stones D & E.
This page; Tullybannocher west stone & Oscar.
Opposite page; Monzie cup & ring stone.
Back cover; Dunruchan stone A, Monzie cup & ring stone.

Published by
One Tree Island Publishing,
Easter Tullybannocher,
Comrie, Perthshire, PH6 2JY

www.onetreeislandpublishing.com

ISBN 978-0-9565499-0-7

Printed in Scotland by Wm Culross & Son Ltd, Coupar Angus

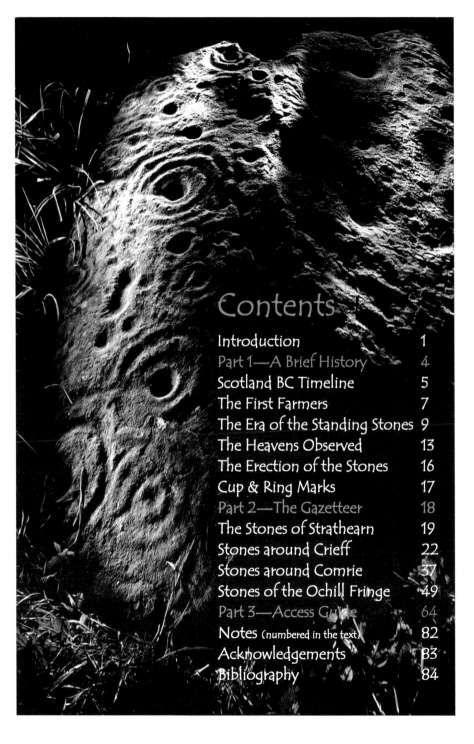

Contents

Introduction	1
Part 1—A Brief History	4
Scotland BC Timeline	5
The First Farmers	7
The Era of the Standing Stones	9
The Heavens Observed	13
The Erection of the Stones	16
Cup & Ring Marks	17
Part 2—The Gazetteer	18
The Stones of Strathearn	19
Stones around Crieff	22
Stones around Comrie	37
Stones of the Ochill Fringe	49
Part 3—Access Guide	64
Notes (numbered in the text)	82
Acknowledgements	83
Bibliography	84

INTRODUCTION

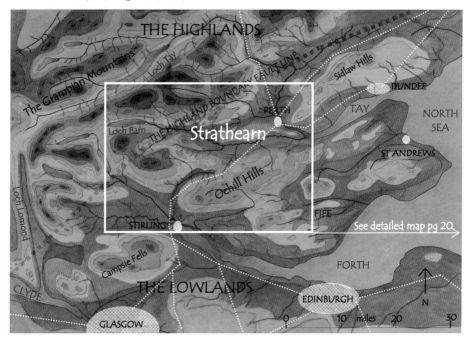

From the Lowlands, highways and byways gather to cross the Forth at Stirling and it is here that northbound visitors, venturers and vanquishing armies have first come into the presence of the Scottish Highlands. As the main north way rises from the Forth basin a wall of mountains fills the horizon from west to north. This is truly the Highland edge for here we see the effects of the Highland Boundary Faultline, a geological tour-de-force, that aeons past ripped diagonally across Scotland. To its north were thrown up the high ice scoured mountain peaks and crystalline escarpments with deep incised lochs that are the predominant feature of the Highlands.

For many modern travellers Strathearn is little more than a fleeting glimpse on the A9 corridor north, but for those who know it better it is an idyllically beautiful and verdant strath with its head and shoulders tucked in amongst superlative mountain scenery. Strathearn remains, in essence, a farming community tending to a rich tapestry of farm fields, woodlands and estates that cloak and grace the Earn basin. It is rich in charm and history boasting, not least, remains of the north west frontier of the Roman Empire etched across its landscape some 1900 years ago.

What is less well known is that in Strathearn there remains the remarkable legacy of an ancient farming community who lived and thrived here some 2 millennia before the Romans arrived. Though thousands of years of the scouring climate and acid soils have reduced much of their remains to little more than stains in the soil there yet stands, as solid as ever, what we call their 'standing stones'.

1

There are many books about standing stones. Some focus on the most evocative 'A-List' sites like Stonehenge, Kilmartin in Argyll, Callannish in the Hebrides or the Orkney Isles. Others cherry pick the nations' most dramatic stones for illustration in coffee table fare. Some are dry and academic whilst shed loads of others spiral into speculative forays in otherworldliness. This book simply sets out to be a gazetteer and guide book to all of the known remaining standing stones in one topographical area and illustrates 38 sites in and around Strathearn.

Driving through the strath it is impossible not to spot some standing stone or other. From the car they may appear as paltry lumps of stone. Close up however things change. The stones themselves are often huge with some over 11 feet high and weighing perhaps 6 tons. Some stand alone and some form part of a complex localised group like the six stones in close proximity on the flank of Dunruchan Hill by Comrie. They stand, more often than not, at the apparent centre of gravity of some glorious amphitheatre of hills and mountains. Furthermore, exploration makes it clear that there are an inordinate number of such sites within a very small locus.

I have tried to avoid speculation and let the stones, photographed in their landscape, speak for themselves but do show, where available, a little archaeology for context and understanding. Whatever these stones are about, the landscape looms large in their reckoning and Strathearn presents a remarkable backdrop where mountain eminences congregate the horizons. In the photographs I have named many of the hills and mountains to make more palpable the interconnections between sites and hope that, in bringing them all together in this book, it is in their totality and web of close connectedness that they speak loudest.

NN 95500 17350 Level-212m(A)
4 Km S.E of COMRIE

BEN VORLICH   BEIN DEARG   BEN HALTON   MOR BHEINN

EAST FROM DUNRUCHAN

An example of the type of format employed in the book to illustrate a stone in context.

2

These stones were erected by some of the earliest farming communities in the strath around 4000 years ago and that they remain standing at all is a testament to the people that built them. With great communal effort, remarkable ingenuity and in a way suffused with their profoundest beliefs these people wilfully created places which functioned at the heart of their communities for perhaps 50 generations. That they remain here in such remarkable abundance and surrounded by the same, largely unspoiled, horizon line is both a remarkable privilege to experience and a considerable responsibility to protect.

Since I started this project 5 years ago a change has begun in this landscape likely to be more visually significant than anything past as armies of wind turbines and pylons marshal at the Eastern ports just over the horizon come to save us from ourselves. This book may then turn out to be a simple eulogy to these remarkable pre-ecotopian horizons.

At the end of the gazetteer I present an access guide which gives the explorer details and ideas on threading together some of the sites into more ambitious walking itineraries. There is no question that if you have the opportunity to visit any group of sites you will come away with the clear understanding that they represent a much more significant entity than merely a sum of their parts.

The book begins with the broadest brushstroke introduction to the context of the stones. I am not an archaeologist so a ramble through the foothills of the bibliography will be required to get any real inkling of the rich and complex history of the thousands of years of farming communities in this country we tend to deride as 'pre-historic' and largely ignore in the scant potted history of our country with which we drill ourselves. These stones represent the very tangible bedrock of our country's history and it is hoped that this small publication might help an appreciation of these ancestors of ours, their legacy and the landscape they revered.

BEN VORLICH   SLEEPING
GODDESS

THE FAULT LINE

SOUTH WEST FROM FOULFORD

Part One – A Brief History

pg

1 Scotland BC Timeline   5
From the Ice Age to the Romans

2 The First Farmers   7
The Neolithic Revolution

3 The Era of the Stones   9
A 2000 year tradition

4 The Heavens Observed   13
Neolithic Astronomy

5 The Erection of Stones   16
Neolithic Engineering

6 Cup & Ring Marks   17
Neolithic Symbols

Remote as these early farmers may seem, in considering a 24 hour timeline representing the 2 million years since our first certain ancestor walked the earth, these stones were erected at 3 minutes to midnight. Moreover new genetic research confirms that the people of the stones are not some vanished, vanquished race but actually our ancestors, the first farmers of the Strath, whose core of sacred beliefs, lasting a little over 2000 years, faltered under an onslaught from the irrevocable forces of climate change and the cyclically consistent ruinous resource management of the tribes of man no matter the idol of favour. [1]

1. Scotland BC Timeline

9000 BC- the last glaciers were melting away to the North of Scotland and human hunter-gatherers were starting to settle on the shores of this sub arctic tundra. As the climate warmed tundra gave way to woodland as trees moved north. Dwarf willow & juniper, then birch and pine, followed over the next two millennia, by hazel, elm, oak and alder.[2] With their coracles and dug out log boats **Mesolithic** (middle stone age) people explored, discovered , hunted and lived in the primeval hinterland for over 200 generations touching the land so lightly that barely a trace of them remains not dissolved in the acid soils or inundated by the massive floods and scourings of climate change through millennia.

5500 BC-Scotland was virtually covered in virgin forest; mixed oak wildwood on the lower ground, Scots pine woodland above and birch and hazel scrub on the North and West fringes. Hunter-gatherer bands may have begun to live a less nomadic, more pastoralist existence blessed with the teeming fish stocks of inshore waters and numerous river systems, the herding of pigs & deer and hunting in the bountiful wildwood or edge clearings for beast, bird and berry.

4000 BC- profound changes appear in the archaeological evidence associated with the more sedentary lifestyle of what is called the **Neolithic** Period (New Stone Age). This was an era when the people of NW Europe moved from being predominantly hunter gatherers to becoming predominantly farmers. With soils rich in nutrients from 3 millennia of forest growth the pollen record shows a marked increase in forest clearance and the first appearance of grain cereals, that catalyst   for what we accord 'The Neolithic Revolution' though, full scale adoption of agriculture occurred over many generations and in some areas, where resources were plentiful, not until the early bronze age. Evidence of major cultural and technological change appears around this time as new things appear everywhere in the archaeological record; substantial landscape monuments (**cairns, cursus, enclosures**), pottery & polished stone axes.

3200 BC- in a time of some major perturbation in the climate a crisis appears to have shaken the beliefs of the early farmers and we find that the majority of Neolithic burial cairns, once the setting of profound communal ritual, are all blocked and their use abandoned. For a period of 30 years massive volcanic activity ensued around Iceland. Pollen analysis shows previously cultivated areas turning to deserted fields beset by scrub & weeds and a steep decline in the radiocarbon evidence from this time seems to mark some calamity. [3]

3193 BC- Tree rings show virtually no growth .

3000 BC- The climate appears optimal; drier and warmer than today. Profound changes in the nature of society are underway and we see the beginnings of the creation of brand new types of places; the great open air circular monuments of earth, wood & stone with the great megaliths that, for us, seem to typify the profound mysteries and unique idiosyncrasies of the ancient cultures of the British Isles.[4]

2250 BC - A time of great social fluidity and mobility partly associated with the welter of technological innovations accorded to the dawning of the Bronze Age.

1500 BC - Blanket peat being laid down across many parts of the country (up to 1.5mts thick) as the climate deteriorates. In response agriculture intensified and the population continued to rise but good soil management was needed to survive. Excess ploughing and other ruinous agricultural practices leads to much soil erosion and the upland farming areas are abandoned. [5]

1159 BC - Icelandic volcano Hekla erupts and we see tree ring growth woefully retarded as the acid rains fell to poison the soil again.[6]

900 BC - Against a background of profound climate change the sites of the great standing stones are finally abandoned and by 500 BC defensive settlements are being built as the martial clash of the Iron Age spreads across the land. Developments in metalwork hint at the first great arms race where daggers, then rapiers and eventually swords are being produced.

THE LAST ICE AGE ENDS

AFTER 2 MILLION YEARS OF REPEATED GLACIATIONS
& PIONEERS ARRIVE.....

Timeline (BC): 9000 · 8000 · 7000 · 6000 · 5000 · 4000 · 3000 · 2000 · 1000 · 0 · AD

Periods: MESOLITHIC · NEOLITHIC · BRONZE · IRON

Animals / Pioneers:
REINDEER
DEER
HUMAN
WOLF
BEAR
BOAR

Trees / Vegetation:
WILLOW
BIRCH
HAZEL
PINE
ELM
OAK
ALDER
WILDWOOD

Environmental events:
SEA RISES TO 50MTS ABOVE TODAYS [7]
SUB ARCTIC TUNDRA [8]
SEA DROPS TO 40MTS BELOW TODAYS [9]
LINK TO IRELAND FLOODS
SEA RISE TO 9MTS ABOVE TODAYS
CANOPY @ AROUND 15 MTS HIGH
LINK TO EUROPE FLOODS
CLIMATE IMPROVES
DOGGER BANK FLOODS
3200-170 ARCTIC VOLCANOS
3193 NO TREE GROWTH
DRIER AND WARMER THAN TODAY
CLIMATE DETERIORATES
PEAT GROWTH
1160 HEKLA VOLCANO

Developments:
PASTORALISM
LANDSCAPE MONUMENTS
POTTERY
CEREAL
POLISHED STONE AXES
STATUS OBJECTS
PLOUGH
METALLURGY
HORSE
WHEEL
UPLANDS ABANDONED
DEFENSIVE SETTLEMENTS BUILT

Monuments:
CHAMBER CAIRNS
CURSUS
ENCLO-SURES
STANDING STONES
CIRCLES
HENGES

> Indicating the scale of the various deluges of the Mesolithic it is poignant to note that remains of whales were found, alongside the mattocs used for butchery, by Blair Drummond, 5 miles West of Stirling suggesting the sea at one time in this period very nearly bisected Scotland between the Forth and Clyde estuaries. [10]

> Following discovery of the post holes of what appears to be aligned timber posts at Stonehenge dating to around 8000 BC it has to be acknowledged that the peoples of the Mesolithic also created landscape monuments though nothing on the scale or with such consistency as became normative in the Neolithic

PERTHSHIRE........	ELSEWHERE.......
CLEAVAN DYKE	MESOPOTAMIAN INDUS
	WEST KENNET
CROFT MORAIG	MAES HOWE
	BRODGAR
NORTH MAINS	CALLANISH
	GIZA PYRAMIDS
	STONEHENGE
	MINOAN
	BABYLONIAN
SANDY ROAD	TUTANKHAMUN
	TROJAN WARS
	RIG VEDA
	SOLOMON
	GREEK
	NAZCA
	ALEXANDER
	ROMAN
	CHRIST

ROMANS INVADE NORTH OF FORTH AD 81-85 & 211-215

AD

"It is in the period between later Neolithic and the Late Bronze Age, from about 3300 to 900 BC, more than a hundred brief generations, people whose lives were no more than glitters of sunlight on a running stream, that stone circles were introduced, became popular, reached into farther, quieter parts and were finally abandoned." **Aubrey Burl** [11]

6

2. The First Farmers

With the dawning of the Neolithic agrarian revolution around 4000BC we sense a revolution in human consciousness as the pioneer farmers adapted to their new circumstance.

"Agriculture...was not regarded as a purely secular enterprise. It lead to a great spiritual awakening that gave people an entirely new understanding of themselves and their world". Karen Armstrong [12]

As these people bound themselves closer to the land in evermore settled existence, domesticating their plants, animals and fundamentally themselves, their existential foothold seems most powerfully manifest in the monuments they began to erect. With huge effort and in a manner imbued with deep significance they built enormous earth works and stone cairns in significant parts of their territory.

Aerial photography indicates mysterious parallel lines running **for well over a mile** across farmlands by Meikleour (nr Blairgowrie) between the Tay and Isla Rivers in Perthshire. Excavations have revealed a wide central bank up to 20m across formed between two ditches dug around **4000BC** across previously farmed land. Known as a **CURSUS** these 'monuments' are considered to have had some profound function in acting as a ritual focus for local communities and astronomical alignments are often noted. These structures are increasingly coming to light with evidence of around 10 in Perth & Kinross the most recent being a north south cursus found in 2006 beside Crieff High School in an archaeological prelude to development .

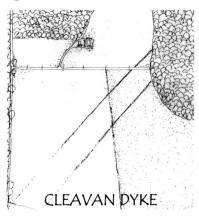

CLEAVAN DYKE

My drawing, based on an aerial photograph, tries to convey the enormous scale of this 6000 year old 'sacred' construction running diagonally across the frame. The modern roadway runs horizontally across the top third and a farm steading, with some half a dozen buildings, sits midway above this.

Deep within often massive piled stone **CAIRNS**, in wooden or stone chambers, were laid the disarticulated bones of their ancestors reached by some low passage aligned often on the midwinter rising sun or other significant celestial event. Scotland's largest Neolithic cairn is in Callander and measures some 1050ft long.[13] The evolution in the types of these early cairns is complex and varies greatly with location but broadly seems to start with single celled family vaults in the middle of the 5th millennium BC progressing to more complicated chambered cairns, acting as clan mausolea, through the 4th millennium BC reaching ultimate sophistication with the court cairns constructed from around **3500-3200BC** where ceremonies seemed to focus in the courtyards beside the cairn perhaps a precursor of the later open stone circles.

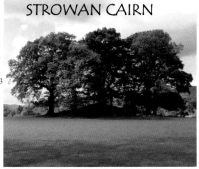

STROWAN CAIRN

Over time most cairns have been stripped of their stone for farm dykes and yet, around Strathearn, many a copse conceals the scant remains of a Neolithic cairn.

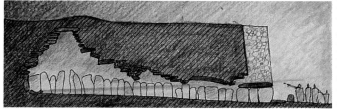

Lest we underestimate the cult of the chambered cairns witness the cairn at Newgrange on Irelands' East coast. Much of the entrance façade was faced with quartz from the Wicklow Mountains 40 miles east and above the entrance a small light box was formed down which only the rising mid-winter sun shone to illuminate a decorated stone basin in the back alcove.

At the edge of the wildwoods in Strathearn their HOUSES would likely be formed in low timber staves placed a pace apart and woven with fresh and pliant hazel, tight like a basket, then plastered with a mixture of turf, mud, straw or dung. A roof of long poles, perhaps coppiced oak would have been woven with hazel, lashed with honeysuckle rope and thatched with bundles of reeds from the copious wetland margins.

The homes of these early farmers may have been modest but a recent chance discovery of 'Balbridie Hall' shows that the **COMMUNAL BUILDING** achievements of these people were considerable. About **3600BC** the people of Strathdee built a great timber hall 86ft long by 43ft wide. My sketch was prepared from a cut away model now in the British Museum. A similar structure has now been discovered by Callander so it seems possible that another such building lies under our feet in Strathearn.

These people would likely have been blessed with fertile farming land at the edge of virgin forests burgeoning in wild foods. They would have had an encyclopaedic knowledge of the flora & fauna and had considerable craft skills like basket weaving, leather work, wood & bone carving. Little remains of their houses or crafts but we do have a tantalising glimpse into their levels of sophistication when we witness their stone carvings. Their cup and ring marked rocks and carved stone balls are little short of mesmerising considering they were fashioned in an age before metal.

The fist sized Neolithic carved balls are a phenomenon almost entirely 'Scottish' in provenance. The ball to the far left was found in the Tay River by Perth and the others a random sample of the 400 or so balls found in the country. (PSAS)

3. The Era of the Standing Stones

Following the climatic perturbations and attendant crisis of the previous 2 centuries by **3000BC** the weather appears optimal; drier and warmer than today. Around this time, in the Orkney Islands, people conceived and built the massive and spectacular Maes Howe and the stone rings of Brodgar & Stenness with an estimated construction times of 100, 80 & 40 thousand working hours respectively.[14] There is a suggestion that a new strong religious impulse testified by such massive standing stone encrusted ceremonial centres, embracing astronomical phenomenon and associated with ritual use of new high status Grooved Ware pottery, originated in Orkney. Perhaps like Iona aeons later this liminal island, through some quirk of geography, kept a potent ember of religious adherence alive in a time of attendant chaos and, in the awakening, became a well spring of innovations in belief. Over the next five centuries or so the building of great centralising open air circular henge monuments with standing stones and associated with rituals and burials involving Orkney style pottery appear over much of the country. Whether the fashion prevailed as an attraction to incipient chieftainships keen to concentrate power or was swept along by powerful communal ideologies is more difficult to . judge.

Across the British Isles and Brittany these new innovative, open air monuments were being created. In Perthshire around **3000 BC** excavations have revealed that 14 timber posts were being erected in a horseshoe setting 8x7m at the north east end of Loch Tay, **CROFT MORAIG** by Aberfeldy. Surrounded by a ditch these posts were then adjusted over generations before being replaced with 8 stones, enclosed by a stony bank and finally embellished with a 12m circle of 12 further stones. Excavations like these tell us much about the processes of transformation that might have lead to the final stone settings we witness elsewhere today.[15]

Much evidence is now coming to light of the many timber constructions of this era. Archaeology confirms that around **2700 BC** people stood on an open terrace just above the Earn at **NORTH MAINS** by Kinkell Bridge and conceived the building of an awesome structure. They dug a 7m wide ditch 2-3 m deep forming a broadly circular platform 30m across. They threw up the spoil from the ditch to form a massive enclosing earthwork some 9m wide and 2 m high. Entrance causeways were left to east and west. Inside this henge they erected 24 large posts forming a broadly circular ring 27 m across flattened on its north side. The posts are likely to have stood 5-7m (16-23ft) tall and may have been subtly graded in height towards some point of the horizon. My sketch section through the henge hopes to convey something of the scale of this place and trigger imaginings of how the space might have been experienced as the shadows of the sun or moon wove patterns across the space. It is not known whether the poles were carved as totems, colour daubed or garlanded.[16]

Around **2250BC** was a time of greater social fluidity and mobility partly associated with the welter of technological innovations accorded to the dawning of the **BRONZE AGE**. Copper then bronze arrived to supplant flint as what had been, for millennia, the tool of choice. Ploughing developed, agriculture intensified, the horse was introduced to Britain and then the wheel. Many of the old ways, with their centralising tendencies, seem to have faltered. The 'universal' ritualised use of Grooved Ware ended and varying regional identities seemed to burgeon. The architecture of new standing stones sites and their associated rituals became more varied across the country as groups perhaps sought to reinforce their localised identities and strengthen tribal bonds by consciously distinguishing themselves from others. Still great circles were built but now burials of both inhumation or cremation were accompanied either by finely decorated **Beaker** pottery (the finest of bronze age pots with strong cultural links to the Netherlands and Rhineland) or by Food Vessels (a type of clay ware developed from indigenous tradition). Special grave goods of this time testify both to the long distance exchange networks now weaving through society and to the increasing role of status and social division within society. Such special items might include fine bronze daggers, jet beads from Whitby (as found at Clathick), Amber rings from the Baltic, Axe heads of Jadite from the Alps (one was found at Lochearnhead though the example below was found at Methlick in Aberdeenshire) fine tools of lignite shale or polished flint where the distance an object travelled likely added to it's talismanic potency. Axes from the Killin 'axe factory' of Creag na Caillich have been found as far afield as Buckinghamshire.[17]

JET BEADS   N.M.S   JADITE AXEHEAD   UNIVERSITY of ABERDEEN   BEAKER POT   1   PSAS

In 1934 Margaret Crichton Mitchell analysed the early bronze age 'Beaker' pottery of Scotland cataloguing around 300 examples. At that time the notion held that these were the product of an invading 'Beaker People' bringing metallurgy from the Rhineland. Genetic analysis now tells us that, by and large, we are the same people we were before the coming of agriculture and whilst the exquisitely crafted leather work, woollens, bone tools and timbercraft have vanished to dust the decoration on these pots remain as rhythmic ciphers to the sense of the tribal identity of their creators.

PSAS

10

By **1800 BC** the evidence points to less energy being expended in the creation of the great ceremonial centres and more on secular field systems and boundaries. The climate was deteriorating with more rain and a temperature of 2^0C below the levels of 3000BC.[19] By **1500BC** we note rapid growth of blanket peat to previously farmed land and much localised erosion of the thin soils causing many upland areas to be abandoned. By around **900BC** the sites of the Standing Stones were abandoned.

Aeons of weather have largely worn down the earth and timber works to little more than stains in the soil now to be seen only from the air as crop marks or on bended knee from the point of a trowel. Countless numbers of the great stones have been hauled down, exploded or buried. Yet, like some studded hem peeking from the layered historical fabric of our current landscape, beguiling concentrations of these stones remain. Unique to this corner of Europe (Britain, Ireland and Brittany) over 1300 standing stone circles were catalogued by Aubrey Burl in 2000. This number does not include sacred places defined by single or more random settings of standing stones. In the Strathearn area, for example, only 11 of the 38 sites identified in this book are catalogued as stone circles.[20]

Stonehenge may be the most famous of the remaining stone circles but is like some cockatoo amongst the sparrows. With its lintelled uprights and mortice & tenon joints it is a showy crossbreed built late in the period, with much fashioning, in stone as if in wood. Standing stones elsewhere appear less elaborate. They may be modest 'boulders' of under a ton or great heavy monoliths of tens of tons set, in some significant part of the landscape, in a wide variety of **patterns** (800 of the catalogued sites are circles, 300 are flattened circles and ellipses, the rest are egg shapes or compound rings) ; **numbers** (there appears a liking for 12 stone rings but great regional variation eg 70% of the primary recumbent stone circles of north east Scotland had 11 or 12 principal stones whilst in Perthshire there is a preponderance of 4 & 8-stone circles) and **sizes** (Avebury's 100 megaliths stood in a circle some 400 m across whilst some circles are only a few paces across.

For two millennia, through and despite much manifest change, some core belief focused great communal effort and ingenuity in the erection of standing stones in the creation & use of places significant to the people who used them. These places were clearly used for gatherings where much ritual activity ensued and wherein the mysteries of death were somehow addressed. To us this best resembles our notion of church and it is alluring to see these places as Cathedrals with star spangled ceilings. What we miss in this understanding is the notion that, in the Neolithic mind, there is likely to have been no easy compartmentalisation of the sacred and the profane. Death, of course, loomed larger for them than it does for us. Increasing population density, living close to livestock and eating from unglazed pottery ware all took their toll with average lifespan of around 33 for men and 28 for women with only a 5% chance of exceeding 45 years of age.[21]

REMAINING STONE CIRCLES BY COUNTRY Showing some County 'Hot Spots'	
SCOTLAND	**508**
Aberdeenshire	130
Perthshire	78
Inverness	32
Hebrides	26
Kincardine	21
Arran	19
Kirkcudbright	19
Banffshire	18
Caithness	15
Dumfries	15
Angus	14
Sutherland	14
Moray	13
Roxburgh	10
Wigtown	9
Argyll	8
Fife	7
IRELAND	**343**
Cork (S.West)	103
Tyrone (North)	89
ENGLAND	**316**
Devon	73
Cornwall	38
Cumberland	38
Yorkshire	32
Derbyshire	31
WALES	**81**
BRITTANY	**49**
TOTAL	**1303**

Scotland is clearly the worlds 'hot spot' for Stone Circles with Perthshire & Aberdeenshire accounting for around 40% of its total.

Archaeology now paints a fuller, more complex picture of the use of these places. Small groups might have regular contact with local shrines but have more seasonal visits to higher order ceremonial centres to meet, exchange news, arrange marriages, deal livestock, dispense & receive justice, be healed or exchange goods. Cattle herding remained the core of the economy with disperse bands coming together seasonally at central ceremonial complexes. Evidence from some sites suggests Autumn gatherings of people and livestock. Some stone circles are considered to have been centres in the axe distribution network where the trade in such 'special' goods was likely imbued with potent symbolism.

Aside from the more exotic axe heads flint was the best material for forming the many stone tools used by Neolithic people but in some areas where this was scant, like Strathearn, other stones such as quartz would substitute. Quartz ,with it's 'magical' properties, also seems an intrinsic ritualised component of these sites. Among the crystalline escarpments of the Highland Boundary Faultline there are many seams of quartz.

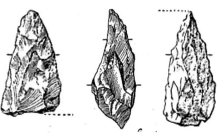

Quartz arrowhead ,axe & awl from Moor of Ardoch
PSAS

Prehistoric highways appear to converge in a meaningful way on many sites often giving the sense of them being portals or markers between significant territories. Sites regularly appear as parts of an extended landscape complex of significant ritual purpose components, perhaps, in songline type narratives once woven across the landscape. Hinting at the ephemeral joys of song & dance likely to have graced these places we know that 200 years ago, by tradition, on the night before May Day in the hills above Callander folks would cut a big turf circle, light a great bonfire and engage in celebration steeped in ancient mythological potency.[22] A Neolithic beaker found in a cist in Fife likely contained an alcoholic beverage, sweetened with meadow-sweet flowers, and it has been noted that often such beakers were decorated with the imprint of hemp plants. In Balfrag, in Fife, a Neolithic bowl was found with residue of black henbane, deadly nightshade and hemlock creating a doubtless powerful hallucinogen echoing a formula in the 1560 *Magiae Naturalis* for a witches flying potion.[23]

We are also aware that great numbers of these stones performed some function in observing the heavens and in doing so perhaps calibrating time itself. Standing, as if at the centre of some huge chronometer, these stones witnessed celestial bodies sweeping like the hands of a clock across the arc of their horizon .

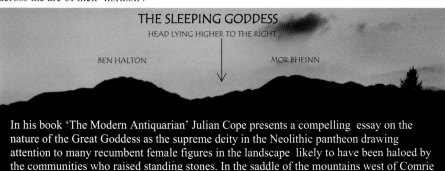

THE SLEEPING GODDESS
HEAD LYING HIGHER TO THE RIGHT

BEN HALTON   MOR BHEINN

In his book 'The Modern Antiquarian' Julian Cope presents a compelling essay on the nature of the Great Goddess as the supreme deity in the Neolithic pantheon drawing attention to many recumbent female figures in the landscape likely to have been haloed by the communities who raised standing stones. In the saddle of the mountains west of Comrie lies a figure known locally as 'The Sleeping Warrior'. Seen from many of the stones of Strathearn this figure may indeed have been 'The Sleeping Goddess' of old.

12

4. The Heavens Observed

The passage of time may, on the surface, appear as the very regular heartbeat of existence. Its deeper conundrums have, however, rarely failed to intrigue, beguile and befuddle the civilising instincts of human beings through the ages set on establishing some order from the vagaries of an indifferent cosmos. We have noted that the early Neolithic peoples (the cairn builders) placed great store in the movement of the sun and saw, in its yearly and consistent transit of the horizon, a metaphor for the cycle of life, death and rebirth central to their beliefs. With the era of the standing stones it becomes apparent that the observation of celestial movements became all the more rigorous.

The essence of the conundrum posed by the heavens is that our definition of time rests on three heavenly bodies whose movements do not neatly correlate. The earth rotates once on axis and we call this a day but its voyage around the sun cannot be expressed in whole days (about 365.24 days) so our definitions of a year, it's equinoxes and solstices, end up as being approximations needing regular untidy recalibrations. The period from one full moon to the next is equally beset with mathematical untidiness (29.53 days) so our months need adjustment to neatly fit our years. More bewildering still on successive nights the moon rise progresses from north to south & back and this oscillation increases in amplitude through an 18.61 year cycle. At its 'major standstill', during the course of one 29 day cycle, it rises from it's most northerly AND its most southerly points (where it appears to skim the horizon). 9.3 years later at its 'minor standstill' it rises & sets within its narrowest confines. Throughout history civilisations have religiously tried to assert some pattern to these seemingly capricious heavenly markers of time and establish a calendar. For farming communities embedded wisdoms are codified into their calendar and the celebration of birthdays, holy days, feast days and anniversaries are part of the essential weave of any society's identity.

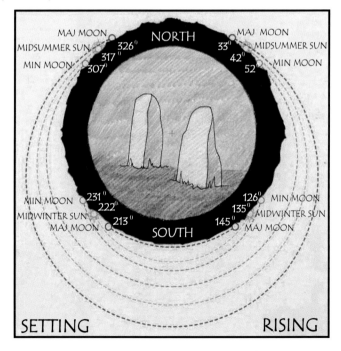

'...beyond the land of the Celts there lies in the ocean an island...inhabited by Hyperboreans..and there is..both a magnificent sacred precinct..and a notable temple...spherical in shape...The moon as viewed from this island appears to be but a little distance from the earth..and the god visits the island every 19 years and...dances continuously through the night until the rising of the Pleiades'

Diodorus Siculus 21 BCE

At the wondrous standing stone 'temple' at Callanish on the Isle of Lewis, once every 18.61 years at its most southerly major standstill, the moon skims low across the horizon then disappears behind the horizon outcrop of Cnoc an Tursa for a few minutes before bursting into light at the foot of the great central stone and casting its beam down the Central Avenue. This is one of the numerous key celestial events cast dramatically here in stone.[24] Before the stones, and for a period likely to be some few hundred years, wooden structures were erected marking and remarking celestial observations until a complete understanding of the heavens was choreographed into a stone temple that then functioned for some 15 centuries.

From many of the standing stone sites we get evidence of careful observation and planning over generations as a prelude to the erection of stones and get the tantalising impression that these early astronomers thus fathomed much of the science which the history books ascribe to later 'civilised' Mediterranean cultures. John Edwin Wood in his book 'The Sun, Moon and Standing Stones' convincingly postulates that the creators of these 'observatory temples' used the mathematical construct of extrapolation and hence utilised 'zero' as a concept hitherto considered invented by the great Arab or Hindu mathematicians of the 8th Century AD.[25] The Roman Empire had no such concept and made do with their unwieldy zeroless number system.

If we are to make anything of the efforts of these ancient peoples to so accurately fix these zero points to which the celestial orbs perpetually return we should reflect on the great circles of Celtic cosmology. We understand that every culture adopts beliefs in a tiered cosmos where cold conscious reality is but one level. Death or afterlife another level and so on. For the Celts this world and the 'other' worlds each ran in independent circles but that, at auspicious moments, these circles touched and for a spell all worlds became one, all time became now and the powers and magic of the Gods and the ancestors became manifest in the mortals realm. These were times of great festival. In their mastery of the wheel of time we must conclude that the ancients corralled many auspicious moments in their sacred places and in so doing created, for themselves, the firmest of existential footholds.

One morning before dawn I chanced a visit to the stones at Tullybannocher to watch a maximum moon setting amongst the craggy escarpments of Crappich Hill. Walking out into the open field amongst the great amphitheatre of hills I always get the impression, on reaching the stones, of arriving at the centre of gravity of this huge space.

In the summer months of 1774 Nevil Maskelyne, Astronomer Royal, camped on Schehallion and conducted experiments with weights hanging off opposite steep flanks in the first 'proof' of Newton's Law of Gravitation showing that mountains had a measurable gravitational pull. He called his report **'The Attraction of Mountains'.**

Standing some little way off I watched as the moon set between the rifle fore-sight I made of the two stones. I was delighted to notice that this alignment also captured the stone circle that was Druim na Cille half way up the hill a mile or so north west. It was then I felt warmth on the back of my neck and behind me the sun was rising from the shoulder of the Lennoch Hill. I ran west beyond the stones and looking back saw the great orb rising, again as if by design, out of the cleft between the two stones. I walked back to the centre of the stones and stood with the moon setting on my right shoulder the sun rising on my left wide awake to the notion that exactly here and at exactly this moment I was palpably at the centre of some overwhelming vastness. This may have been the merest glimpse of part of the *genius loci* of this place.

Likewise it is inescapable that visiting standing stones at auspicious times of the year you are often witness to some aesthetically pleasing celestial event seemingly dovetailed into the very fabric of the place

From the centre of the platform by the great stone on Aoidann Moor the midwinter sun appears to roll down the flank of Dunruchan Hill and set in the cleft formed with Ben Clach

From the centre of the stones at Tullybannocher the mid winter sun rolls down the slope of Little Tomanour Hill and sets in the cleft at the foot of Ben Halton

15

5. The Erection of Stones.

"The rings were not erected in a haphazard plan, nor were their stones casually discovered. Each was part of an intended design. The Materials and structure of a circle were as significant to their builders as the nave, choir, altar,... were to the masons and priests of the Christian Church. But the builders of the stone circles were illiterate. They left no bible except for the stones"   Aubrey Burl

In conceiving the great stone circle at Old Keig in Aberdeenshire some ancient tribe selected, as their great alter piece stone ('recumbent stone'), a block of sillimanite gneiss weighing about 53 tons which they had to transport from its source in the Don Valley some 6 miles away. This was a task that would have demanded ingenuity, coordination and the strength of over a hundred people. With the smaller stones of some few tons no less so were their skills engaged. Following 1933 excavations at Old Keig stone circle in Aberdeenshire H.E Kilbride-Jones set out a theory about the ingenuity involved in the erection of standing stones[26] He observed that the monoliths had been quarried and thereafter shaped, with pounding from stone mauls, to a definite predetermined form and that this was done, in part, to lessen the thrust necessary for their erection. Stones would then have been moved by timber rollers and skids perhaps aided with honeysuckle ropes. He noted that the apex of a standing stone was rarely above the centre but in line with the 'vertical' side and the opposite 'curved' side stopped short so the stone tapered to a point at the base.

  In expressing the theory of the erection in mathematical terms it was demonstrated that, to erect a 5 ton monolith as the diagram below, the thrust required in direction T would only be around 1.5 tons and that this thrust reduces to zero when the centre of gravity of the stone reaches the line AB. Once balancing on its toe the stone would have been back wedged with stones and, with relative ease, nudged to it's intended alignment then the excavation back filled.

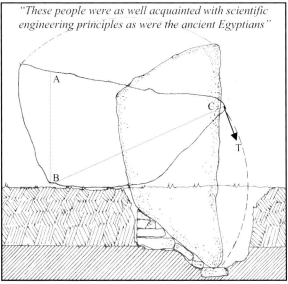

"These people were as well acquainted with scientific engineering principles as were the ancient Egyptians"

My drawing showing notional erection of stone Pm from
Old Keig Stone Circle (borrowing from HE Kilbride-Jones)

16

6. Cup & Ring Marks

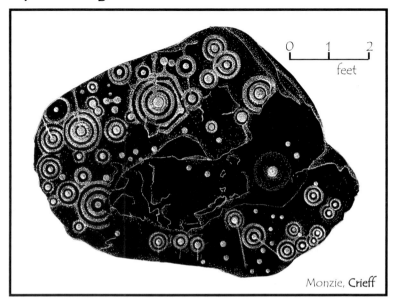

Monzie, **Crieff**

Lomba de Costa **Portugal**

Carschenna, **Switzerland**

Across Europe, in the Neolithic Period, people were making uncannily similar cup & ring symbols pecked with stone tools into stone surfaces. Some are on loose slabs of stone often incorporated into dark burial chambers. Some are at higher vantage points often cut into bare natural rock outcrops. They generally associate with cairns and standing stones and loosely associate with numerous other phenomena to the extent that any clear and definitive understanding of their meaning remains elusive.

There appear to be as many theories are there are cup & ring marks but I will rudely précis some in a paragraph; They are **maps** of , burials, metal ore deposits, water springs, territories, cosmology or the underworld. They are **templates** for jewellery, augury, healing, games. They are **computations** of land, stock, lineage or time. They are **narratives,** allegories, songs & songlines. They are **magic**, they are energy, they are pictures of the gods.

Whatever they are, they do say something and thus represent the earliest communication we have from our ancient ancestors though the pleasing babble of indecipherable circles and the allure of a profound mystery will meantime have to suffice.

Part Two - A Gazetteer

	pg
The Stones of Strathearn	19
Stones Around Crieff	22
Stones Around Comrie	37
Stones of the Ochill Fringe	50

The Stones of Strathearn

Strathearn lies in an area of remarkable geological and topographical contrast where an abrupt change in the landscape is defined by one of the largest features in the earth's crust crossing Scotland: The Highland Boundary Fault Line (HBFL) running from Stonehaven in the North East, across Arran and on to Clare Island off the Atlantic coast of Ireland. It is this line which defines the fundamental division of Scotland into the Highlands and the Lowlands. To the North of the fault ancient crystalline rocks of metamorphic type predominate uplifted in great tectonic plate movements 4-500 million years ago. To the South lie younger sedimentary formations. Forming the Southern wall of the Strath the Ochills are predominantly basalt and andesite lavas folded parallel to the HBFL.

The hard and varied rocks of the Highlands were more resistant to the scourings and clawings of the ice sheets as they advanced and retreated during glaciations so rugged peaks and deep incised glens and lochs feature. The softer rock to the south has been worn to a more gentle landscape coated by the residue left in the trail of ice and the deluge of melt waters. The fault line is still active. In a 500 day period from the violent 4.9 scale quake of October 1839 247 earthquake occurrences were noted in Comrie.

The standing stone sites of Perthshire are considered to be late examples in the megalithic tradition supported by radio carbon (r.c.) evidence from Sandy Road in Perth indicating dates of 1650-1300 BC though it has to be noted that r.c. evidence shows that the Stone circle at Croft Moraig by Aberfeldy began life as a timber circle around 3000 BC. Aubrey Burl, Britain's foremost authority on stone circles, notes that the ceremonies conducted here in Strathearn are akin to those evident in north east Scotland and that the monuments themselves are strongly related with those in both Argyll and around Inverness. This is explained as being the result of some cultural continuity, with ancestry in the east of Ireland, linking a broad south west to north east band hundreds of miles long running diagonally across Scotland and Ireland somewhat echoing the Highland Boundary Fault. Strathearn can thus be seen as lying on some prehistoric highway along which people and ideas flowed over millennia.[27]

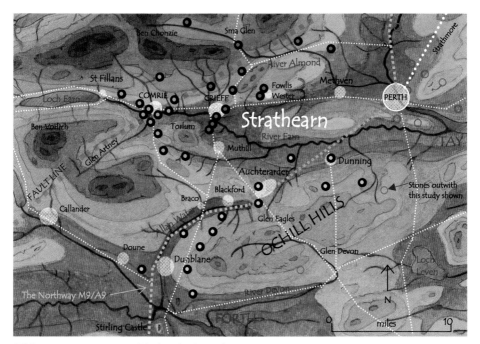

This gazetteer presents 38 sites in 3 sections ;

- Stones Around Crieff -13 sites - pg 22
- Stones Around Comrie -12 sites - pg 37
- Stones of the Ochill Fringe -13 sites - pg 49

The Earn runs from its deep mountain bound loch in the west to be joined by the Ruchill and Lednock in a cauldron of sparkling waters in Comrie then below Crieff, between the eminences of Torlum and the Knock, and out across the broad behummocked Strath to join the Tay just below Perth in the east. The mountains of the Highland Boundary Fault run from south west to north east.

Parallel and to the south, the wall of the Ochill Hills contains the strath. The long history of Crieff acting as a tryst town for cattle drovers testifies to its prime location at the hub of many ancient routes at the very boundary between the Highlands and the Lowlands. Routes from the south cross the Forth at Stirling and run north up the deep fissure of the Sma Glen to Aberfeldy and Dunkeld or up through Strathmore to Aberdeen. Glen Eagles cuts south through the Ochill Hills connecting to Fife.

It should be noted that to the west of this map there are no standing stones for about 40 miles . To the south only a handful are to be found till the Southern Uplands some 40 miles off and, to the east, Fife & Kinross together have around 20 sites. The rich seam of stones in Strathearn is however echoed in the stones of Strathtay and Strathmore to the north and north east.

This book's title might properly have included Strathallan and Strathalmond but I allow myself the simplification as Strathearn appears to be the centre of gravity of this particular concentration of standing stones.

It must also be noted that the maps I paint are somewhat abstracted hence for armchair appreciation only and cannot be used for guidance in the real world where there is no substitute for the relevant OS maps.

20

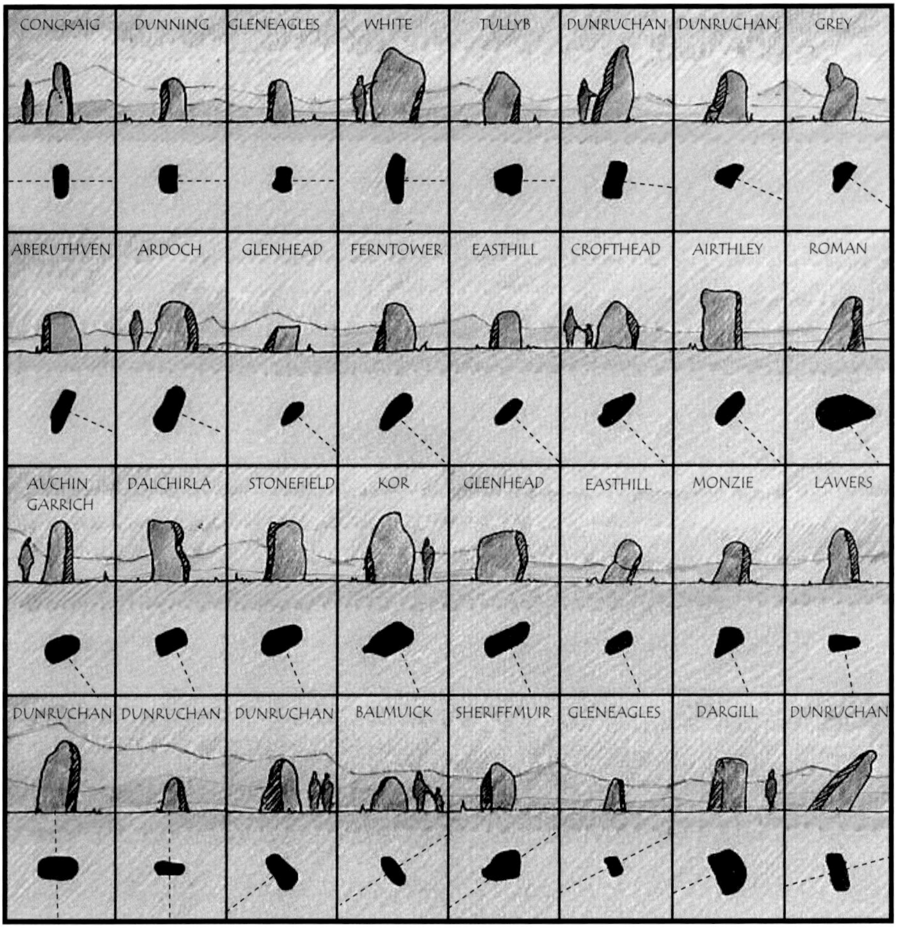

CONCRAIG | DUNNING | GLENEAGLES | WHITE | TULLYB | DUNRUCHAN | DUNRUCHAN | GREY

ABERUTHVEN | ARDOCH | GLENHEAD | FERNTOWER | EASTHILL | CROFTHEAD | AIRTHLEY | ROMAN

AUCHIN GARRICH | DALCHIRLA | STONEFIELD | KOR | GLENHEAD | EASTHILL | MONZIE | LAWERS

DUNRUCHAN | DUNRUCHAN | DUNRUCHAN | BALMUICK | SHERIFFMUIR | GLENEAGLES | DARGILL | DUNRUCHAN

In the area of this study there are 49 stones still standing and around 40 others fallen and lying in-situ or removed within recent recorded history. Many more lie buried by time, hauled off and ditched by farmers or exploded, broken and disappeared by zealots of many eras. The diagram above shows 32 examples of the stones. Some are red sandstones while others are blue metamorphic rock. The scale is indicated by the doodled humans nearby. In the plans, as in the rest of the book, north is up.

With a dash of speculation and a dashed line I have shown the direction the stones appear to be facing. This appearance extrapolates to suggest half face broadly south east (+ or -12°) and a quarter appear to be on an east-west or north-south axis. The application of some rigorous archaeo-astronomy may, in time, reveal more about these fixed points set amidst the perpetual revolution of the heavens. The apparently wilful orientation of these stones hint at the observation of heavenly bodies rising or setting over hallowed horizons corralling and calibrating the passage of time and the synchronising of calendar days.

21

Stones Around Crieff

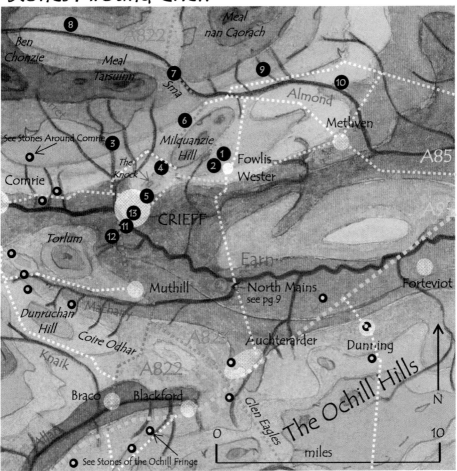

1	MOOR of ARDOCH	245m	I start this section with The Moor of Ardoch
2	CROFTHEAD	165m	stones above Fowlis Wester not least because
3	STONEFIELD	228m	the site has some interesting archaeological
4	MONZIE	118m	evidence which helps provide early illumina-
5	FERNTOWER	135m	tion of the subject generally.
6	FULFORD	220m	The sites vary greatly in altitude with the last
7	CLACH OSSIAN	205m	three down on low fields by the river.
8	CLACH na TIOMPAN	270m	Crieff lies at the heart of this area spread
9	KOR STONE	195m	across the southern flank of the Knock above
10	LYNEDOCH	100m	the Earn. It has for aeons been a crossing point
11	DARGILL	37m	of routes from the four points of the compass
12	CONCRAIG	45m	and hence a place of ancient tryst.
13	DUCHLAGE	50m	

① MOOR of ARDOCH

NN 92300 24950 Level-243m
1.0 Km NNW of FOWLIS WESTER

THE OCHILLS

SHERIFF MUIR   COIRE ODHAR   TORLUM

B

D

C

A

SOUTH WEST ACROSS THE STRATH

An east west track rides the north rim of the Strath out across the Moor of Ardoch above Fowlis Wester. It is here, on this glorious promontory where the moor ridge ends with the little hillock of Shian (fairy mound), that a sacred place was built. From here the whole strath lies at your feet from the broad lands of the Tay estuary in the east to the mountain pass of Lochearn in the west. To the north east long views across the face of the Highland Boundary Fault open to Little Glenshee and the Blairgowrie Hills. This is an exceptional spot from which to watch the long sky roll across the strath, it is easily accessible and, with the light cast by an archaeological dig here in 1943, presents an ideal introduction to the area.

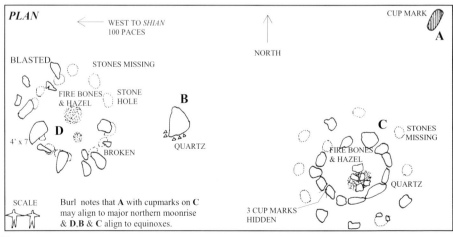

PLAN

← WEST TO *SHIAN*
100 PACES

CUP MARK

A

NORTH

BLASTED   STONES MISSING

FIRE BONES   STONE
& HAZEL   HOLE

B

D

QUARTZ

C   STONES
MISSING

4' x 7'

BROKEN

FIRE BONES
& HAZEL

QUARTZ

SCALE   Burl notes that **A** with cupmarks on **C**
may align to major northern moonrise
& **D,B** & **C** align to equinoxes.

3 CUP MARKS
HIDDEN

23

AN ARCHAEOLOGICAL DIG BY ALISON YOUNG IN 1943 N0TED :

A-Standing stone of schistose stone (6'0" above ground buried 2'0") appears to stand on mound. To the east burnt bone, charcoal & greasy black 'earth' mixed with quartz pieces. To the west side a row of large white water worn stones had been carefully placed just below the ground. **B**-Massive (9'0"x7'5") fallen whinstone with quartz pieces. **C**-Double ring setting of stones. The outer ring stones were bedded in the natural earth strata(see section below). 3 cup marks lie hidden below ground in the south west quarter. A pavement of clay & small stones was laid level across the central ring. Burnt bone fragment and hazel charcoal lay scattered with patches of greasy black 'earth' mainly in two scoops in the clay floor. All the boulder sockets contained black 'earth' and quartz pieces. The central bone/quartz deposits were covered with stones. The whole circle was then likely built over with hand stones to form a cairn (now denuded to the benefit of local stone dykes) With the standing stone (A) probably represents the oldest grouping. Kerbs stones appear graded W-WSW. **D**-Circle of once standing stones 24'0" across all fallen, blasted, broken or missing. Ritual activity inside with fine scatterings of burnt bone and hazel charcoal. Appears as a later addition to the group and less well built than (**C**).

A SECTION THROUGH CAIRN CIRCLE C

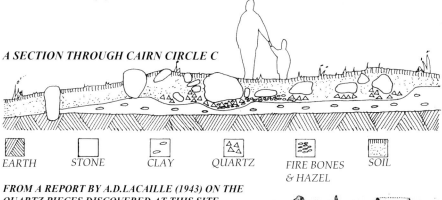

EARTH	STONE	CLAY	QUARTZ	FIRE BONES & HAZEL	SOIL

FROM A REPORT BY A.D.LACAILLE (1943) ON THE QUARTZ PIECES DISCOVERED AT THIS SITE

"..We are confronted with the products of a fully developed industry...little workshop debris recognisable...(therefore) it must be inferred that the quartz implements were chosen for incorporation. The manufacturers were exponents of a lithic craft.. (with)..ancestry in western Mesolithic cultures (south western Scotland and Northern Ireland)

AWL   ARROW HEAD

PSAS

NORTH EAST OVER GLEN ALMOND

2 CROFTHEAD

NN 92050 23900 Level-165m
0.7 Km West of FOWLIS WESTER

WEST

Two large erect blue whinstones sit on a slight mound by a small burn on the southern slopes of the Braes of Fowlis between the farms of Crofthead and Thorn. The stones are of distinctly differing shapes ; the west being flat faced and angular like some huge arrowhead whilst the east is curvatious. 100m or so to the south east lie two massive natural boulders each around 4m in length. The southernmost of a diorite like material shows remarkably deep and narrow channels. The northmost granite boulder displays three cup marks.

NORTH WEST TO STANDING STONES

3 STONEFIELD

NN 85200 25050 Level-228m
3.0 Km NNW of CRIEFF

MILQUANZIE HILL
BREAS OF FOWLIS
KATE MCNIVENS CRAIG
MONZIE
THE KNOCK

ESE THROUGH TO THE STRATH & THE OCHILLS BEYOND

Up on the flanks of the breas of Monzievaird, above the confluence of the Turret, Barvick, Keltie and Shaggie Burns, tucked in behind The Knock away from the full glare of the strath, this grassy platform hosts a massive blue whinstone standing proud 8'3" high & 6'3" wide. The flat south eastern flank cuts a line across the landscape from the caves of Skirley Craig in the north east to the Glen Artney gap over Comrie in the south west as it will remain when the shackling iron gates are dust.

TORLUM
GLEN ARTNEY

SOUTH WEST TO THE GLEN ARTNEY GAP

SKIRLEY CRAIG

NORTH EAST TO SKIRLEY CRAIG

26

As glaciers retreated north up the Shaggie & Turret Burns the deluge of melt waters deposited sand and gravel into a natural amphitheatre forming this broad 100 acre terrace above the Earn basin. Out on this terrace in the thrall of Kate McNivens Craig and Milquanzie Hill you will come upon an unassuming huddle of low stones forming a rough circle with a large, recumbent cup and ring marked stone 5m south west. 300m to the west (between the two foreground trees) a standing stone stands alone.

PLAN

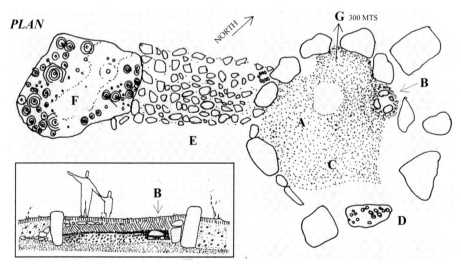

Plan, section and following notes based on the report of a 1938 excavation by Alison Young FAA Scot & Margaret Crichton Mitchell MA PhD FSA Scot

A- The remains of a kerb cairn. The area had originally been stripped so as to present a compact floor of sand. Ten large stones were bedded in the sand with their broad faces on the arc of a circle 17'0" in diameter. Big lumps of quartz were closely packed at stone bases.

B- A burial cist was laid enclosed by green waterworn stones to north & south and red felsite stones on the east & west. The cist was packed with comminuted burnt bone (The remains of an adult & child aged 6-8yrs) and quartz. A cover stone of volcanic diorite was placed and the cist was packed around with sweet herbage.

C- A black layer of 1"-5" covered most of the circle. This layer contained bone fragments and hazel charcoal defined by a thin red crust suggesting extensive fire.

D- A 4'0" deep block of schistose grit carved on the top with deep cuts & connecting channels.

E- A 'causeway' of stones.

F- A metamorphosed grit boulder covered with cup & concentric ring marks.

G- Standing stone 300 yds yest.

A rim sherd found at the site had affinities with pottery found at Old Keig stone circle in Aberdeenshire.

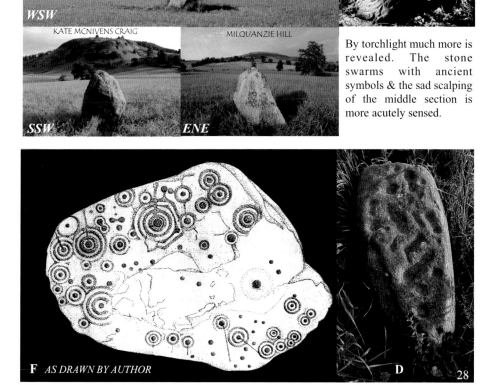

Standing stone with its flat face parallel to the Highland Boundary Fault running South West in the Shaggie Burn 500 m beyond

GLENTURRET

F

WSW

KATE MCNIVENS CRAIG

MILQUANZIE HILL

By torchlight much more is revealed. The stone swarms with ancient symbols & the sad scalping of the middle section is more acutely sensed.

SSW

ENE

F *AS DRAWN BY AUTHOR*

D

28

5 FERNTOWER

NN 87400 22600 Level-135m
North East edge of CRIEFF

MILQUANZIE HILL

BREAS OF FOWLIS

NORTH EAST

Above Crieff on its north east edge, in the thrall of Milquanzie Hill and saddled between The Knock & Callum's Hill, these stones look out over far horizons to the south east and south west. In 1910 F.R.Cole noted.. "4 stones of quartz seamed whinstone & diorite in an almost true circle of 27'6" diameter. East stands a great erect whinstone monolith 6'5" tall beside a block of reddish schist."

COIRE ODHAR   TORLUM

SOUTH WEST

OUTLIER

200m ESE of the main grouping, on the south side of the main road, a small outlier stone stands by the dyke. (thanks to David Cowan for re-discovering this little kent stane)

29   **EAST**

NORTH WEST

BEN VORLICH

FAULT LINE

VIEW FROM FOULFORD LOOKING SOUTH WEST

CRAIG KIPMACLYNE

SKIRLEY CRAIG

Stone opposite the Foulford Inn with as many as 60 cup marks on its surface.

NN 89950 27000 Level-220m

MILQUANZIE HILL   THE OCHILLS

MONZIE

NN 88100 27400 Level355m

Although there are no stones still standing here, where the ancient route from the north descends down into the Strath from the Sma Glen, there is much to intrigue and beguile the modern antiquarian. Within a 1 km radius on the Braes of Monzie lie 5 stones with many cups and ring marks & three cairns.

The stone bottom right lies 2km off by a peak in the Bracketrigg Hills where nearby lies what looks much like a fallen standing stone.

TORLUM

SKIRLEY CRAIG

NN 88100 27550 Level378m

NN 88000 27400 Level355m

CRAIG KIPMACLYNE

NN 88700 26350 Level225m

THE OCHILLS

NN 91100 26000 Level320m

DUN MOR

BRACKETRIGGS HILLS

OSSIAN'S STONE

SOUTH EAST DOWN THE SMA GLEN

The river Almond winds its way across the narrow fields on the floor of the impressively steep sided Sma Glen. Immediately below the steepest crags of Dun Mor to the east, the boulder strewn flanks of Meall Tarsuinn to the west and close where the ancient route way and river touch a great megalith stands. It was brought by the ice, haloed by the early farmers, nudged by General Wade and venerated as the resting place of the mythic bard Ossian.

DUN MOR

EAST

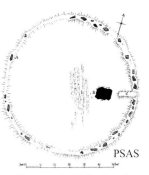

PSAS

F.R.Cole recorded the site in 1910 and made this drawing. This site and the great cairn on the summit of the western slope are variously said to hold the revered bones of the great bard Ossian. In 1732 the Chronicles of Strathearn noted that the stone had lain directly in the line of General Wade's road and was moved over by 'vast labour'. Where it stood they found a small stone lined cist with burnt bone and metal artefacts which Cole concluded was '..the burial of a prehistoric hero of earlier date than that ascribed to Ossian'

8 CLACH na TIOMPAN
CROM CHREAG

NN 82900 32800 Level-*270m*
12Km NNW of **CRIEFF**

COIRE GARBH

WSW ACROSS THE RIVER ALMOND

4 miles up Wester Glen Almond beyond Newton Bridge a blue quartz riven whinstone stands to the south of the track on a little circular ridge above the river. Presumed to be the last of a group the stone's broad face looks WNW down the glen and is aligned, on it's long axis, to the peak of Eagle's Rock to the SSE.

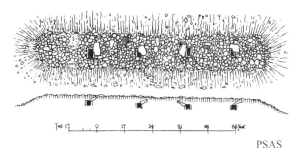

PSAS

Adjacent to the north lies the remains of a cairn unusually long at around 53m. 4 large oblong cists are exposed each with a great covering stone lying askew. In 1910 F.R.Coles prepared this sketch of the cairn. The map notes the remains of a stone circle 300 m west in the field by the river.

EAGLE'S ROCK

SSE

CROM CHREAG

STUCK CHAPEL CRAIG

WEST ACROSS THE CAIRN

32

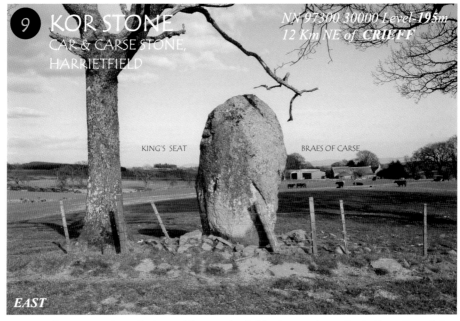

KING'S SEAT

BRAES OF CARSE

EAST

Up on the Braes of Logiealmond by Harrietfield, above where the Milton Burn joins with the river Almond, a great ten foot high, six ton whinstone stands on this grassy platform with long views east to Kings's Seat in the Sidlaw Hills and west to the Glen Artney gap and Vorlich.

MILQUANZIE HILL   VORLICH

GLEN ALMOND

° In 1910 F.R.Cole noted that the Statistical Account states that there were three other stones in the vicinity and that the west pillar of the Druminnor stone circle is Aberdeenshire is also known as the Kor Stone.

SOUTH WEST

NO 303500 728900 Level-*100m*
3 Km NE of *METHVEN*

SMA GLEN

WEST STONE
1000M AWAY ON
GRASSY PLATEAU
BEYOND WOOD

EAST STONE NORTH WEST

Three similar stones each a little over four feet tall stand 500m apart strung across what appears an old river trough a few hundred metres from the River Almond . Apart from glimpses west the sites have mostly tree clad horizons but a short walk to intriguing knolls and hummocks adjacent to the north rewards with panoramic views to the north east up Strathmore and South across the Ochills.

MIDDLE STONE NORTH EAST

WEST STONE NORTH EAST   34

11 DARGILL

NN 85900 20050 Level-37m
1 Km South of CRIEFF

SOUTH EAST

NORTH NORTH EAST

NORTH

This monolith stands on a broad gravel terrace on the south bank of the Earn by Dargill Island. Torlum lies close to the west and long panoramas open to the south east and the north. J.R Coles noted "...up to 1909 two other great stones were standing. The remaining megalith is an unusually square and massive oblong of schist, girthing over 16' and standing 7'8" in height"

35

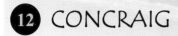

KNOCK MARY

TORLUM

WEST

Like a hand raised in prayer this stone of conglomerate red sand-stone faces Torlum with it's flat back. It stands about 7 feet high in this broad field above the Balloch Burn with long views north and glimpses to the distant east through a cleft in the landscape.

SOUTH   *EAST*

13 DUCHLAGE

In 1910 F.R.Cole prepared this drawing looking west. The stone stood , by the road, where the skate board facility serves the new Community Campus. A dozen paces or so into the field south of the road, and at the end of a cursus, stood a Neolithic mound cairn. Latterly known as the 'Stayt' mound, it went on to become Crieff's principal place of judgment until 1665. The mound was levelled for plough in 1860 when a clay urn and two burial cists were uncovered. [28]

PSAS

36

Stones Around Comrie

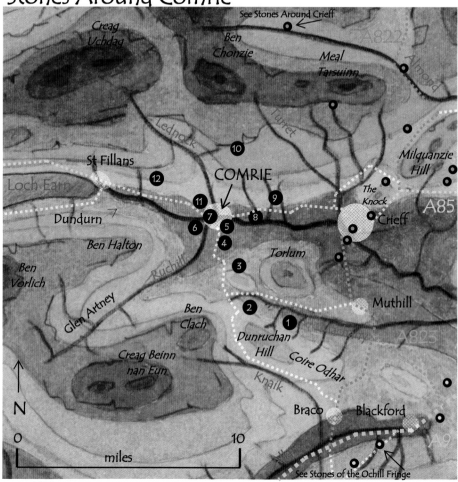

1	DALCHIRLA	121m
2	DUNRUCHAN	212m
3	AUCHINGARRICH	135m
4	ROMAN STONE	65m
5	DUNMOID	60m
6	CRAGGISH	68m
7	TOM na CHESSAIG	65m
8	LAWERS	53m
9	CLATHICK	125m
10	BALMUIK	352m
11	TULLYBANNOCHER	65m
12	DRUIM na CILLE	195m

This section begins with the the intriguing alignment at Dalchirla then up to the complex of 6 megaliths spread out over 1km on the north flank of Dunruchan Hill before venturing down into Comrie across the Earn and out onto the south facing hill sides for the remaining stones. Comrie (translated as 'the confluence of the waters') is at the heart of this area nestling below mountain eminences with its head and shoulders in the glens.

1 DALCHIRLA

NN-82450 15900   Level-*121m*
NN-82300 16100
4 Km East of **MUTHILL**

LURGAN HILL

WEST STONE

EAST STONES -NORTH WEST

Down on the flat fields of this quiet little glen, tucked between Torlum and the north flank of Coire Odhar, down where the Machany Burn runs east to the Earn there sits this intriguing complex of stones. To the east stand a pair of red schist stones, one curvaceous and 8 feet tall the other angular and squat. Some 300 m to the north west a single 9 feet shard of stone stands hemmed by field stones.

TORLUM

WEST STONE -NORTH

COIRE ODHAR

WEST STONE -SOUTH

In 1910 F.R.Cole made this drawing of the West stone and noted that the pair resembled groupings at Edintain & Fonab Moor

PSAS

38

② DUNRUCHAN

NN 95500 17350 Level-212m(A)
4 Km S.E of COMRIE

CRAIG ROSSIE THE OCHILLS

(A) SOUTH EAST

Up on a roughly circular platform on the north flank of Dunruchan Hill stands the tallest of the Stones of Strathearn (A) 11'6" tall this schist block stands like some other worldy sentinel gazing across a spectacular panorama; south east to the Ochills or north west to the craggy escarpments of the Vorlich range. Another 5 standing stones share this hillside.(B) -(F)

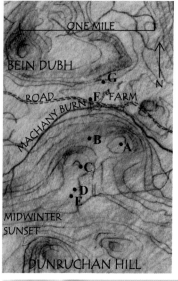

ONE MILE

BEIN DUBH

.G

N

ROAD •F FARM

MACHANY BURN

•B •A

•C

•D
•E

MIDWINTER
SUNSET

DUNRUCHAN HILL

At Midwinter the long shadow hand of the great stone touches the edge of the platform

(A) NORTH

At Midwinter the sun rolls down the flank of Dunruchan and sets in the cleft to the right. DUNRUCHAN HILL

(A) SOUTH

BEN VORLICH BEN HALTON

BEINN DUBH

(A) NORTH WEST

Stone C—a vast pinnacle of red schist 12 feet along its top edge and 6 feet broad at the base stands below a small knoll.   LEVEL 229m

THE OCHILLS

(C) S.EAST

on the first horizon C   LEVEL 198m

DUNRUCHAN HILL

(B) SOUTH

This 9'9" monolith stands and stares north in quiet vigil over it's cairn.   LEVEL 231m

C

(D) NORTH EAST

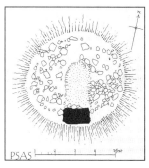

PSAS

LEVEL 231m

D   A

LURGAN HILL

(E) NORTH EAST

F.R Cole prepared this drawing of stone D in 1910 noting "..a stony cairn or platform 15ft in diameter. Stone E stands on the west arc of a rudely circular setting. ..Numerous small, low cairns are scattered about...to the east of Stone E...(by the stream) another great stone lying prostrate.."

LEVEL 160m

Also known as the Craignelch Stone

(F) WEST

LEVEL 170m

(G) NORTH

Behind the farm lies an impressive stone outcrop with a cup mark on top.

40

3 AUCHINGARRICH

NN 78700 19600 Level-135m
1.5 Km S. of COMRIE

BARR DUBH

LURGAN HILL

SOUTH EAST

This 8'7" tall block of red schist sits on a grassy knoll in the middle of Auchingarrich Wildlife Park at the low end of Glentarf. The hills to the south and east attend closely. To the north and west spectacular views are now eclipsed by the park buildings. Some compensation is to be found in the café.

CAFE

WEST

BEIN DUBH

Two of the cup and ring marked stones of Glentarf & Glasscorrie recently rediscovered & photographed by 'Tiompan'.

SOUTH WEST

41

GLEN ARTNEY   BEN HALTON   MOR BHEINN   BIORAN DALHONZIE

WEST

A traveller from the south, descending off the Coire Odhar and passing Dunruchan & Auchingarrich, arrives down on to the Earn River basin into this most majestic of amphitheatres. To the east the Earn and the fault line sweeps towards The Knock over rich alluvial fields. To the north and west the mountainous edge of the fault line rears up in a geological fanfare of granite intrusions and crystalline escarpments. This massive, characterful stone and attendant cup marked stone lie atumble by the road in what was, in the first century AD, the inner rampart of a large Roman camp so they may have moved some from their post of the prior two millennia. Ancient burial tumuli are gathered 600 m South West by the Water of Ruchill. (These are the 'great cairns' referred to in ⑩)

THE KNOCK

SOUTH WEST   *EAST*   *NORTH WEST*

In 1910 F.R.Cole made these drawings & noted.. "a great rough block of what seems like diorite A... & a smooth rounded boulder C covered with 22 neatly made cups"

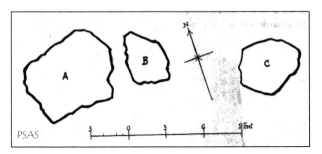

PSAS

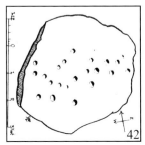

NN 78000 21200 Level-60m
S.E. EDGE of COMRIE

SOUTH

On a roundel in the woods by the Comrie Cemetery lies this group of four stones
where only one remains standing. The spot is called Dunmoid or Mound of Judgment.

SOUTH EAST

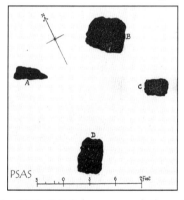

PSAS

In 1910 F.R.Coles prepared these two
drawings. The view west to Ben Halton
shows two stones standing. The plan
shows a circular setting of some 15'0"
diameter where stones A & C are reddish
schist whilst B is of whinstone. He notes of
some digging and disruption on the site
which discovered a stone cist in front of
the largest slab containing a thigh bone
and a separate find of an urn filled with
ashes.

43

PSSA

6 CRAGGISH

BEN HALTON   BIORAN DALHONZIE

LITTLE PORT HILL

SITE OF STONES

WEST

CARN CHOIS   BALMUICK

MILQUANZIE HILL

THE WHINNEY STRIP

TOM na CHESSAIG

NORTH EAST

In perhaps the most expansive amphitheatre setting of all this site has been wantonly bereft of its megaliths. The 1896 OS map shows 2 lines of 3 stones. They stood, by the road, in what is now 'The Whinney Strip' a boulder strewn strip of land 20m wide dividing up otherwise flat and even grazing land.

7 TOM na CHESSAIG
HILL OF ST KESSOG

NN 77000 22050 Level-65m
WESTERN EDGE of COMRIE

TOM na CHESSAIG

In 1910 FR Cole noted aural history confirming several great stones forming a circular group on the little hillock by the Earn adjacent to the present Church of Scotland.

NORTH EAST

8 **LAWERS**

BEN HALTON

WEST TOWARDS COMRIE

Down on the Carse of Lennoch on the broad fields by the Earn stands this single curvatious whinstone monolith with it's broad southern face in Torlum's thrall. Its long axis lines east to The Knock and west to Ben Halton. From here the 'Sleeping Goddess' can be seen lying in the saddle between Ben Halton and Mhor Bheinn to the right. The Clathick stone would once have been seen on the braes of the north eastern horizon.

LAWERS HOUSE

NORTH   *SOUTH*

9 CLATHICK

NN 81150 23200 Level-125m
3km ENE of COMRIE

NORTH

On a small platform outcrop above a tumbling burn this quartz veined shard of stone lies akilter showing at its head the swirl and weave of it's metamorphic creation frozen in stone. Torlum dominates the backdrop with views far south east to the Ochills and west to Ben Halton & the Glen Artney gap.

TORLUM

SOUTH

46

⑩ BALMUICK

*NN 78350 25200 Level-352m
3 Km N.N.W. of COMRIE*

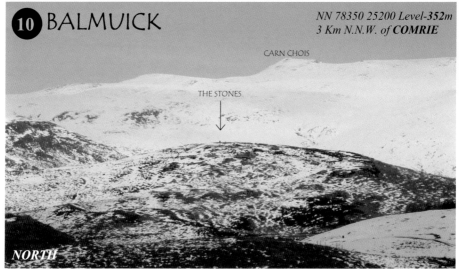

CARN CHOIS

THE STONES

NORTH

High on a hummock on the wide lonely moorlands below the summit of Carn Chois six stones lie in an irregular group with only one still standing. Views are broad and long from the south east to the north west. Ancient cairns nestle in nearby woods.

CARN CHOIS

DUNRUCHAN

ABERUCHILL HILLS

COMRIE

S S W

NORTH EAST

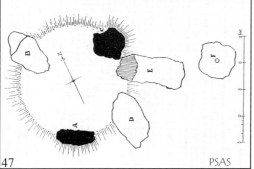

47

PSAS

In 1910 F.F.Cole made this drawing and noted..a stone setting rudely circular in form around 12'6" dia. Stone B-whinstone, C-schistose, D&F-Granite. 'The interior of the circle is smooth, very slightly concave with a circumference made up of a low ridge of small boulder stones. The prospect on all sides is magnificent and looking south westwards we can decry, amongst other prehistoric sites, three great cairns on the right bank of the Ruchill.'

SOUTH WEST WINTER SUNSET

From Comrie westbound the road zig-zags with the Earn between the rocky hummocks of Twenty Shilling Wood & Easter Tullybannocher and out into this broad swathe of farmland. These two stones sit in what feels like the centre of gravity of a majestic amphitheatre of hills and mountains. The west stone is angular with three distinct faces the east stone more irregular with a cup mark.

DRUIM na CHILLE
CRAPPICH HILL

NORTH WEST

BEN HALTON   MHOR BHEINN

RIVER EARN

THE STONES

BEN HALTON

F.R.Coles writes in 1910 that there were origi-nally four stones shown in old maps then three until 1893 when one was removed by the farmer as plough obstruction. The west stone is of quartziferous schist, the east of whin-stone. The broad sides of the stones face NE and NW inferring the removed stones stood on the northern arc. Professor Thom noted sig-nificant lunar alignments.

From here, at mid winter, the sun rolls down the flank of Little Tomanour Hill to set in the cleft at the foot of Ben Halton

The three faces of the west stone.

NORTH WEST

SOUTH WEST

NORTH   48

12 DRUIM na CILLE

BIORAN BEAG

CAIRN CIRCLE

WEST

On a high south facing plateau below the craggy escarpments of Crappich Hill & Craig Liath this glorious place lies by the ancient Maarm Road that leads over the mountain pass to Lochearn in the west. The cairn circle commands a broad panorama from east to west across upper Strathearn and a row of megaliths lie sadly where they were pushed in the recent past.

DUNRUCHAN

TULLYBANNOCHER

SOUTH EAST

The fallen stones cup-marked foremost

WEST

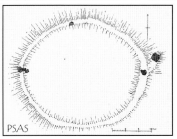

PSAS

In 1910 F.R.Cole prepared this drawing and noted..'a cairn circle enclosing a space about 34 feet in diameter. 25yds to the east a whinstone with 13 beautifully clear cut cups and 5 other blocks of considerable size..rumours that these were once set in a circle around the cup marked boulder.'

The site is associated with the burials of unbaptised infants whose souls were ostracized by a cold hearted Christian orthodoxy.

The story goes that the past owner of the estate who had these stones pulled down thereafter befell great family misfortune.

Amongst the high crags of Crappich Hill a quartz outcrop 12m by 2.5m is clearly seen from the Maam Road and from the Tullybannocher stones far below on the river basin.

49

Stones of the Ochill Fringe

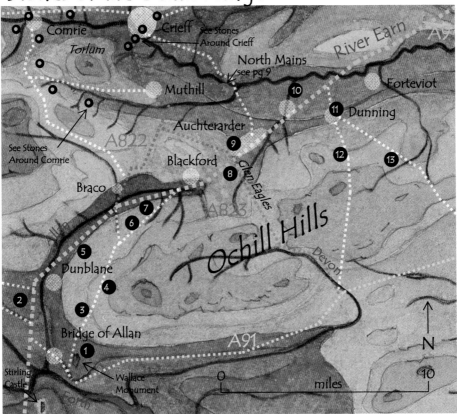

1	AIRTHREY	35m
2	CUPAR LAW	110m
3	SHERIFFMUIR	310m
4	GLENHEAD	274m
5	WHITE STONE	150m
6	WESTER BIGGS	260m
7	BOAT STONE	212m
8	GLENEAGLES	140m
9	EASTHILL	125m
10	ABERUTHVEN	32m
11	DUNNING	52m
12	GREY STONE	252m
13	PATHSTRUIE	190m

These sites are strung out in a loose line some 20 miles long as are the principal towns of Doune, Dunblane, Blackford, Auchterarder and Dunning. Again the elevation of the sites varies from the high hill flanks of Sheriffmuir to the riverside terrace of Aberuthven.

The section begins with the southernmost stones by Bridge of Allan and then travels north east to visit the stones straddling the main north way.

I have neglected three sites of previously standing stones on the southern edge of Perth and one forlorn stone by the police station in Stirling which might otherwise have extended this section but were finally considered out with the nexus of this book.

50

① AIRTHREY

STIRLING UNIVERSITY

NS 81400 96500 Level-35m
1 Km E. of BRIDGE of ALLAN

DUMYAT

CASTLE LAW

NORTH WEST

Up on a playing field plateau on the south west shoulder of the Ochills and in thrall of the Wallace Monument this great megalith faces south where panoramic views open over the Forth Basin and east along the southern escarpments of the Ochills. Half a mile north west a towering peculiarity, like one stone homunculus on another's shoulders, looms from the flank of a wooded knoll.

CASTLE LAW

THE SOUTHERN
FACE OF THE
OCHILL HILLS

KNOCK
HILL

EAST

NS 80600 96850 Level-35m

WALLACE
MONUMENT

SOUTH WEST

51

BEN LOMOND   BEN LEDI

NORTH WEST

CUPARLAW

SOUTH WEST from Sheriffmuir Stone B

A small hillock on the westmost rump of the Ochills hosts a massive red stone slab likely to have once stood around 10 feet high. The great eminence of Dumyat stands close by. Panoramas open wide to the south over Stirling and west & north up the broad swathe of the Forth river system to its headwaters amongst the distant mountains of the Highland Boundary Fault Line.

LOSS HILL   DUMYAT

SOUTH EAST

52

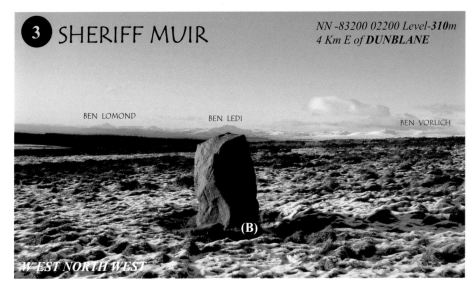

BEN LOMOND   BEN LEDI   BEN VORLICH

(B)

WEST NORTH WEST

Opening on to the broad expanse of Sheriffmuir & amidst the bloody clashes of recent history, five stones stretch quietly in a line for some 300m along the flanks of the Old Wharry Burn attending some north eastern point on the racking horizon of Glentye Hill. Only one stone, **B** -The 'Wallace Stone', remains standing. Stones **A,B & D** are clearly aligned with fallen stones **C & E** being a few feet askew. Up here the mountain grandeur of the Highland Line fills the horizon from north to west. The face of stone B aligns broadly towards the stone of Cupar Law 3 Km south west.

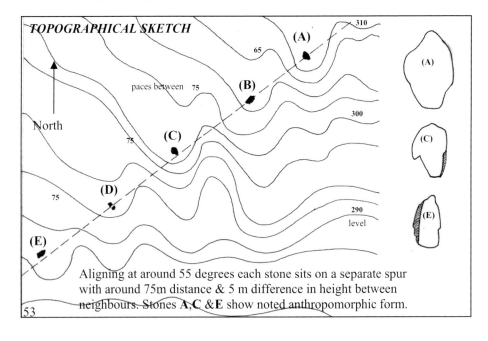

TOPOGRAPHICAL SKETCH

310

(A)

65

(A)

paces between 75 **(B)**

300

North

75 **(C)**

(C)

(D)

75

290
level

(E)

(E)

Aligning at around 55 degrees each stone sits on a separate spur with around 75m distance & 5 m difference in height between neighbours. Stones **A,C &E** show noted anthropomorphic form.

(B)

GLEN TYE HILL

(C)

(D)

NORTH EAST

GARGUNNOCK HILLS

Fallen stone with over a dozen cup marks

(E)

SOUTH WEST

BIG HUNT HILL

(A)

EAST

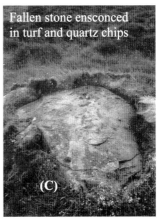

Fallen stone ensconced in turf and quartz chips

(C)

54

BEN LOMOND

BEN LEDI

BEN VORLICH

NORTH WEST

SSW

NORTH WEST

Just off the brow of a little knoll on the braes over Doune this place, with its flat topped, cup marked centre stone and flanking megaliths, sits like some alter setting before the great sweep of the Forth and Tieth rivers into the mountains deep in the north & west. East, beyond the brow of the knoll, Dumyat stands majestic as an end piece to the Ochills.

600 m north a great megalith stands alone by the edge of a wood above the Ardoch Burn in some aligning gesture of enormous antiquity. Further up the burn on the Braes of Doune Cromlix Long Cairn and Judges Cairn have attended south eastern horizons far longer still.

CUPARLAW

DUMYAT

ESE

5 WHITE STONE

NN 80600 04200 Level-150m
2 Km N.E of DUNBLANE

SOUTH WEST

COIRE ODHAR

NNW

Travelling from the south, as the A9 rises from the Forth basin around the western flank of the Ochills, the unsuspecting traveller may glance to the east and see this stone stand inconspicuously in the fields edging Sheriffmuir. Close up however this is a impressively large blue whinstone slab, lying slightly a-kilter at over 10 feet high and 6 feet broad. This massive slab was raised to align north south striking a line towards Cupar Law now eclipsed by trees and shows, on it's southern lower edge, a bold chamfer cut common to many of the stones vestigial perhaps of the engineering of its erection.

BEN LEDI

BEN LOMOND

WEST

6 WESTER BIGGS

BEN VORLICH

BEN LEDI

WNW

By Wester Biggs the OS map notes a stone circle. There is nothing obvious left here. No stones, no circle, just an unerring sense of closeness to the sky and the attraction of mountains

Out along Sheriffmuir (near Harperstone Farm) the view to the north and east opens up to the (snow capped) fringe of the Fault Line. Here we get our first glimpse of Torlum peeking above the Choire Odhar ridgeway (the Langside) that runs out from Gleneagles towards Comrie and the Earn and forms a watershed between the Forth and Earn tributaries.

BEN CLACH   BEN CHONZIE   GLEN TURRET

CHOIRE ODHAR   TORLUM

NNW

7 BOAT STONE

NN 87200 04100 Level 242m
2.5Km S.E. of BLACKFORD

SOUTH WEST

SOUTH

The road drops down from Sheriffmuir and by some woods near Blackford a quartz veined stone lies fallen in a field close by. Its shape is akin to Sheriffmuir stones A,C & E and connects by happenstance or design to the alignment of the two stones at Gleneagles some 6km ENE and the White Stone 7km WSW.

HAWK CRAIG   EAST CRAIGS   WEST CRAIGS
BEN SHEE

(A)

SOUTH EAST

OCHILLS   (B)   (C)

(A)

W.S.W

(A)

(A)

E.N.E   (B)

The ancient route from Fife leads down through the portal of Gleneagles as it rents the north flank of the Ochills. At the mouth of the glen a 6 feet high quartziferous blue megalith sits on a small promontory (A). On its north west face a symbol of unknown antiquity is cut. A similar smaller symbol can be seen on Dunruchan stone E.

Below, some 350m WSW, towards Peterhead Farm, stands a smaller, rounder stone (B) about 4 feet high.. Here the Allan Water runs east to the Forth and the Ruthven Water west to the Earn. From here the spine of this watershed runs north west to form the Choire Odhar, a natural ridge way to Comrie, making the place feel like a cross-roads.

The alignment of these stones appears to run 6km WSW to the Boatstone (C) & then 7km on to the White Stone.

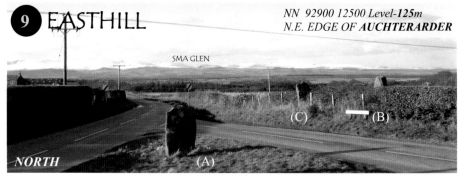

SMA GLEN

(C) (B)

NORTH (A)

On the north edge of Auchterarder roads conjoin amongst these three stones on the north facing braes above the Earn. Stone (A) is unusually waisted like some great capstan. Stone (B) is said to have a carved hand print. The views are long to the Highland Line west & north. Stones (B) & (C) frame long views E.S.E to Kinnoul Hill over Perth.

TORLUM   GLEN TURRET

NORTH WEST   (B)

SOUTH EAST   (A)

KINNOULL HILL

(C) (B)

E.N.E.

CAIRNIE BRAES · DRUMFINN HILL · *EAST*

On a broad terrace above the confluence of the Earn & the Ruthven Water this red sandstone slab sits in the thrall of Craig Rosie with its flat face to the south east and commanding panoramas full circle.

GLEN TURRET · SMA GLEN · *NORTH*

CRAIG ROSSIE · *S.S.W*

SMA GLEN

NORTH

Tucked behind Dunning in the thrall of Craig Rossie and close by the graveyard this six feet high blue whinstone megalith stands with its broad face running north south.

CRAIG ROSSIE

SOUTH WEST

EAST

CLEVAGE HILLS

OCHILLS

E.S.E.

NO 02200 11800 Level-252m
3 Km South of DUNNING

GLEN TURRET

SMA GLEN

NORTH WEST

High up on the North flank of the Ochills over Dunning this extraordinary blue whinstone stands seven feet tall with Strathearn spread below to the west and north. From all angles the shape is evocative not least the view to the north east like some pert nosed Easter Island head.

SIDLAW HILLS

NORTH EAST

EAST

NORTH

Not noted on maps this enigmatic quartz veined megalith sits amongst the hummocks and hillocks of the Ochills on a south east facing hillside above the Water of May with views opening to the south and east. On its eastern flank there appears a deep carving like some great sword hilt.

SOUTH

Part Three- A Guide

	pg
Access to the Stones	65
Stones Around Crieff	67
Stones Around Comrie	71
Stones of the Ochill Fringe	76
Walking with Stones	79
Walking into the Future	81
Notes (as numbered in the text)	82
Acknowledgements	83
Bibliography	84

ACCESS TO THE STONES - A WORK IN PROGRESS

Grouped and numbered as the appear in the gazetteer as follows;

THE STONES AROUND CRIEFF

THE STONES AROUND COMRIE

THE STONES OF THE OCHILL FRINGE

Though these notes often assume that a vehicle needs be part of the formula to deliver you near any particular locus much walking is required and it is hoped that the guide will stimulate the creation and illumination of a variety of walking and cycling routes around numbers of sites. At the end of this section I include some ideas or more ambitious walking itineraries. On my last visit to Foulford, within a 15 minute spell, I watched 7 buzzards spiralling on the thermals above the Monzie stone, 3 red kites, 3 ravens, and a riotous flock of peewits so come replete with binoculars.

By necessity some access arrangements are straightforward but some are vague. Most of the stones stand in private ground, often in fields of crop or beast, some on shooting estates, some by busy roads and a few with easy, unrestricted access. My principal worry in the creation of this guide is that any increase in the popularity of these sites might lead to a conflict with the people who live and work in this beautiful and diligently managed landscape. These stones were erected by the earliest farming communities of the Strath with an unmistakable reverence for the landscape. Remember that you are entering the lands of the current farming community whose respect for their landscape is no less palpable so please pay great heed to all the imprecations of the Countryside Code particularly ;

- *Park only in recognised parking places or with permission. One car may be a small thing in the landscape but it can ruin a whole days work for a farmer.*
- *Keep dogs and children under closest control particularly anywhere near animals. A dog on the loose is a wolf to a sheep and dog tae a coo a red rag to a bull.*
- *Do not galumph over fences and stone dykes as they are expensive and time consuming to repair. A herd of suburban amateur antiquarians scrambling over a stone dyke is as welcome as a farmer and his tractor would be crossing their well tended lawns. Find a gate and use it.*
- *Do not walk amongst a crop and yes grass can be a crop.*
- *Do not wave this guide literally or metaphorically in front of anyone as if it's an admission ticket.*
- *Remember farmers don't just farm but many, like Abercairney Estates , operate conservation of wildlife schemes that can be seriously prejudiced by a few marauding dogs at sensitive times of the year. (eg ground nesting)*
- *Etc. and all the other common sense codes and much more to the extent that folk inspired to visit the stones should borrow an ethic from British mountain climbers who seek to leave no trace. No cigarette ends, not a crust nor a crisp.*

65

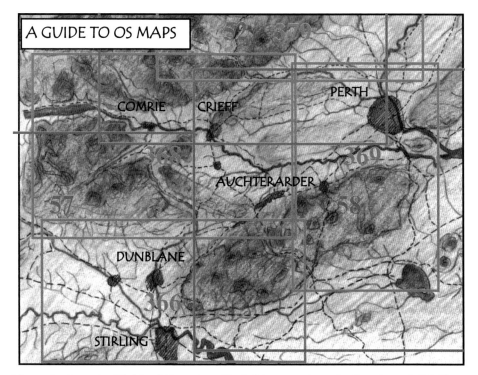

A GUIDE TO OS MAPS

Not only does the Highland Boundary Fault Line run through Comrie and Crieff so too the OS map boundaries. Using either the 1:25000 (orange) or the 1:50000(pink) maps you will need at least 3 maps to cover all the stones in this book. The 1:50000 are better general all purpose maps and extend to well outside the map area above. The 1:25000 benefit from greater detail (marking some cupmark stones & footpaths etc ignored by the pink), 26 out of the 35 site are on one map (368) and that same map allows for better appreciation of context (the 1:50000 infuriating cuts through Comrie and Crieff so much map shuffling is required between otherwise proximate sites.) The table below show which site numbers appear in which map eg the orange map no.379 only shows sites no.8 & no10 around Crieff.

map	showing sites around...	CRIEFF	COMRIE	OCHILLS
	1:25000 Explorer Map (Orange)			
366	Stirling & Ochills West			1-9
368	Crieff Comrie & Glen Artney	1-7, 9 & 11-13	1-12	8-10
369	Perth & Kinross			10-13
379	Dunkeld, Aberfeldy Glen Almond	8&10		
	1:50000 Landranger Map (Pink)			
52	Pitlochry & Crieff	1-11 & 13	4 -12	
57	Stirling & The Trossachs		1-6	1-5
58	Perth & Alloa	1-7 & 10-13		6-13

66

Ideally park in the main square in Fowlis Wester and walk to this site. (After visiting The Parish Church and, inside, two superb 9th century Pictish cross slabs one depicting Jonah and the whale. The stone outside in the square is a replica). Follow the public road North out of the village and up the hill. After 500m the road veers left. After a further 500m, by a farm gate, the view opens out to a track heading off west. Carefully negotiate the gate and follow the track for around 500m. The standing stone is visible to the left and only some 20m off the track. The area is heather moor so nesting birds need consideration. Walk from the stones due west about 100m to the knoll known as Shian (Fairy Mound) where a small burial cist was discovered. From here the stones of CROFTHEAD are visible and the view deep into the west opens up. The remains of a couple of dishevelled outposts of WWII vigilance adorn the ridge and provide occasional respite from the wind.

With time on your hands follow the track down around Loch Mealbrodden and over the Bracketriggs Hills to the Foulford Inn 4km west ,stopping off to see other stones of note (see 6. FOULFORD).

2. CROFTHEAD

From your parking place in the Fowlis Wester village walk out the farm road heading west. 250m after the road end to Crofthead Farm you will see the stones 100m up the field on your right. The fields will be either in crop or being grazed so all the imprecations of the Countryside Code apply. You may be able to walk the burn edge up to the stones. Leaving Fowlis Wester note the burial cairn below a copse of trees by the A85 at the cross-roads.

3. STONEFIELD

Take the A85 west out of Crieff towards Comrie. Before the end of speed limit sign take a right north signposted to The Famous Grouse Experience. In about 800m park by the 20 foot copper Grouse and have an 'experience' at Scotland's oldest distillery. From here walk the road north and 100m over the burn take a left signposted for the Water works. After about 1 km the Barvick Burn cascades down a series of falls on the right. (there is a small parking space you might like to check out before succumbing to the Grouse). Before crossing the burn take the switch back farm track up the hill to the right. After 800m of a steady climb take the track rising steeply on your left and in a little over 100m you will appear out of the woods northern edge. The stone stands in the field about 300m North. This is a shooting estate and a private house lies 200m further north so be considerate.

4. MONZIE

Park safely in Gilmerton and walk the North Road (A822). After about 300m take the left fork for Monzie. 300m again takes you to the east entrance gates to Monzie Castle. The entrance lodge is a private residence so be considerate. The cairn circle and cup & ring marked stone lie to the right of the track some 200 m from the lodge. Follow the track round 300m to view the standing stone.

These fields are often in crop or being grazed so access is limited of necessity. Consult the aerial view of the site on http://maps.live.com and you will see the faint outline of a large circle of around 70m diameter immediately south of the standing stone. This would be a good site to visit walking down from FOULFORD or over from STONEFIELD. To walk to FERNTOWER go back into Gilmerton and take a right on the main road heading for Crieff. Within about 30m, on the right hand side at the sharp bend, a track leads up a switchback and along the southern flank of The Knock and leads south west across the Golf Course. 2.5km from Gilmerton the stones lie about 100m East of the track. The Castle is a private residence but a visit to Monzie Parish Kirk brings rewards ; elegant 1692 gate piers, octagonal bellcote and radiant west window by William Morris and Edward Burne-Jones. Join the public road again by the east lodge and take a left (NNW) .The kirk lies 1km on the right. The river can be seen cascading over two geological fault lines beside the graveyard.

5. FERNTOWER

These stones lie between two holes on Crieff Golf Course so many considerations spring to mind. There are a number of recognised routes through the course so ask a member, or at the Pro Shop, before galumphing across the course.

The game itself involves small rock hard projectiles regularly outwith the control of the participants whose day you could well ruin with any number of breaches in a system of etiquette more akin to a martial art. Be suitably considerate.

In the woods around there are other large stones lurking. The footpath north runs past old Ferntower House and can be followed east to see the Monzie stones some 2km NE. The outlier stone lies behind a stone dyke, by a field gate, on the south side of the A85 500m NE of the Golf Course entrance.

6. FOULFORD

A fabulous place to visit a winter sunset. Take the A822 north out of Gilmerton. There is a handy lay-by about 1km up this road to take in the glorious view across Monzie and west to the mountains at the head of the Strath. From this lay by binoculars will help you study STONEFIELD and MONZIE. 4km up the road pop into the Foulford Inn for refreshment and use their parking. (At the time of printing this book the Inn was closed perhaps irrevocably) Walk 50m north of the Inn and before the 9 hole golf course, take a right and follow the farm track up the West flank of the Bracketriggs Hills. After a little under 2km, reaching the saddle with Miquhanzie Hill to your right (south west), take the track veering left. About 300m south west of the unnamed peak a small cup marked rock lies with splendid aspect across the Strath. At the peak a great stone lies partially buried below a field dyke. This stone is reminiscent of the shape of many of the standing stones around here and may be a fallen megalith.

300m north east of the Foulford Inn a great cup marked stone lies recumbent in a field 40m South of the track. Local Antiquarian David Cowan considers this stone to

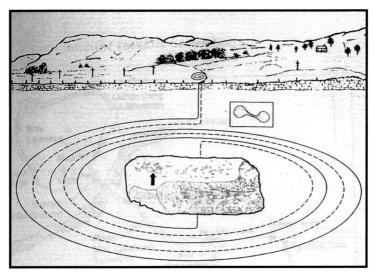

In his book 'An Extraordinary Journey into the Earth's Natural Energy System' Cowan shows 'The primary spiral. A wave is emitted from the stone, spirals around it, then is ejected to the small mound at the top of the picture.' The inset shows the dumb-bell shaped petroglyph (stone carving) said to represent the earth energy circuit looping around this stone and Ben Lawers to the north west

1km back down the A822 south west of the Inn a farm track leads north west to join the Shaggie Burn. 350m from the main road two cup marked rocks lie by the side of the track.

 Walk off the track 50m south west onto a roughly circular platform which would be my candidate for an undiscovered ancient ceremonial site. Intriguing stones and long parallel mounds hint at more recent archaeology. Follow the track west and cross the Shaggie Burn and pause to savour the ozone at the head of a significant water fall. After about 50m take the rough field track to the left and follow this for about 500mts. On the highest knoll before coming to a field gate and dyke you will see a stone reminiscent in shape to many standing stones and having at least two cup marks. Savour the view down to Monzie standing stone to the south. In this area you can also spot iron age hut circles with their entrances facing east to the rising sun. Return to the main road and follow it north east for 100m and take the track on the left to Connachan Farm. 300m up this track a small path to the left takes you the 100m or so to Loch Luig. The remains of a small cairn lie 50m to the south east of the loch. Return to the main track and take a left at the 'cross roads' of tracks 60m beyond the farm. A cup marked stone lies at the left side of the track some 350m from the 'cross-roads'. A further 500m on two cup marked rocks lie 20m to the right of the track. Walking up the hill (off track) due north you will come upon a cairn and within 200m the last of the cup marked rocks of this area.

7. CLACH OSSIAN

Follow the A822 north from Gilmerton. After 6km, on a flat platform of terminal moraine centred on the mouth of the Sma Glen and about 600m east of the junction with the B8063, lies the site of a Roman fort at Fendoch which, around 84AD, would have sheltered a *cohors milliaria* of around 1000 troops in over a dozen buildings in a 200,000 sq ft enclosure. There is an ancient cairn at a level of around 325m on the Bracketriggs Hills behind and another, 'The Giant's Grave', in the woods by the River Almond about 1.5km from the junction. Ossian's Stone lies by the road about 3km north of the junction. There are a few legitimate but lean lay-bys along the road down through this short fissure of a glen. 1km beyond the stone you will find a proper, riverside, picnic spot car park. The field may be grazed so the usual precautions apply. Note the line of General Wade's Military Road of the 1720s & 30s running parallel to the road in the field by the river immediately south of the stone.

8. CLACH na TIOMPAN

Park in the riverside car park on the A822 by Newton Bridge, cross the bridge, immediately take a left and walk the track WNW signposted as a footpath to Loch Tay. The track up this glen is a well maintained estate track so easily walked . Follow the riverside for about 6km up this pretty glen and in about an hour you will come to the standing stone on the road verge and the cairn opposite. 300m west on the field to the left the map notes a stone circle.

Stop at the little graveyard near the stone or walk 500m further west to join The Rob Roy Way, and walk the hills for days. Afterwards drive to Aberfeldy to bask in the loveliness that is the Watermill Bookshop and Café.

9. KOR STONE

Park safely in Harrietfield and ideally refresh yourself at the delightful Harrietfield Inn. 1km west of the village take a private track on the right to Milton Farm. The road goes between private residences and the stone lies 200yds east of the track across a broad field likely to be in crop or grazing so rigorous attention to standard courtesies apply.

10. LYNEDOCH

There may be a walking route from the Harrietfield Inn via the Lodge track beyond Chapelhill but I will here stick to what I know. 2 km NE of Methven the road to Pitcairngreen crosses the Almond at Dalcrue. Immediately over the bridge take a left and, staying right, follow the track for about 1km and safely park by the last (likely desolate) industrial unit and continue up the track on foot. In a few hundred metres you will pass Lynedoch Cottage on your left and should catch site of the middle stone on the hill above and behind the charming derelict steading. The main track veers left. Follow this and stay left and you will come to the west stone on a hillock. From the middle stone follow the contours south east for about 500m and you will come to the east stone. North of both the middle and east stones are knolls with panoramic views south and east.

70

11. DARGILL

About 1km south of the Crieff Bridge and 80 m east of the main Muthill Road this stone stands invariably amidst crops or grazing beasts but can be well seen from a generous access road immediately after the stone on the east side. This is the access road for Scottish Water to attend riverside kit so be sure access is kept clear. Like wise the stone can be glimpsed from the car park of Stuart Crystal with the benefit of coffee and scones on hand.

13.CONCRAIG

Across from Dargill Stone a minor road heads west to The Balloch and the fringes of Torlum. About 600m from the Muthill Road a farm track leads south. 300m down this track you will see the stone 200m east in a field likely in crop or being grazed. Drummond Castle battlements appear above the trees to the south west. A trip to their Renaissance garden may serve as counter point to the rugged moors and primal geometries of the Neolithic.

HAYNES

1. DALCHIRLA   STONES AROUND COMRIE

Visit Muthill and pause for breath at the 12th Century Old Parish Church; a great rarity of a ruin with Romanesque Tower and roofless arcades of aisles evoking a lean ,elevating spirituality to contrast the earth bound trinket box of it's 19th century successor nearby. At the end of Drummond Street the main road turns right and out of the village headed for Crieff. 100 m round the corner take left up the minor road by Muthill Golf Course after 2.5km take first right, then 200m beyond, first left. Just under 1.5km west take the farm track for Dalchirla. The stones lie in the low fields less than 1km from the public road. Down this farm track there are very limited places you might suitably park. The stones lie in fields generally grazed or in crop so access may be limited. Ask someone before venturing out into the field or abandoning your car. Often the landscape appears empty of people but, given patience, you will invariably encounter humans and though often towering intimidatingly down from roaring tractors they tend to be an affable lot unless you are being wantonly stupid. Were it not for an inconsiderate herd of conifers Dunruchan's Stone (A) would be seen on it's platform 3km WNW. An alignment of the stones runs pretty close by 'Dougal's Cairn' 3km south east on the horizon shoulder of Coire Odhar.

2. DUNRUCHAN

From Dalchirla return to the public road and take left (west). After about 4km , 100m after the track to Craigeich Farm, you will happen upon stone F 10m into the field on your right. This is the 'Craigneich Stone'. Alternatively , about 4km from Comrie, up the B827 'Langside', take a left at the Glen Artney crossroads and the Craigneich stone lies to your left after about 1.5km.

There are no ideal places to park as the minor road is quite tight and field gates are much in use by the farmers so park in the lay-by 200m south of the crossroads on the B827 and walk the 2km into Craigneich. From the layby stone D can be seen SE in a cleft tween moor & hill.

The 7 stones range about the hill and can best be navigated using the inset map to the detailed site page. Be aware that the moor is frequently being grazed by sheep or cattle and that some bull or other may not be far from the scene. As you climb the hill the central stone (A) lies hidden from view atop a grassy platform. It is only at the edge of this platform that the stone hoves into view. It is wise to also be prepared for a bull of many tons to likewise hove into view as they seem to favour the locus of the stones. A disturbed bull and an absent minded stone gazer replete with canine chum can be a recipe for macabre comedy.

Driving south up the Langside there comes a point, looking from Middleton Farm's road end, you will see the two south west stones of the complex framing a recumbent stone to the sky.

1km north of the crossroads, at Bishopfauld farm a convincing menhir decorates the entrance.

3. AUCHINGARRICH
2km south of Comrie or 1.5km down from the GlenArtney crossroads on the B827 enter the Auchingarrich Wildlife Park, go the 500m up to the reception/café and pay to go in to nuzzle with the animals or go to the café for tea & scones and sweet talk the lovely proprietor to let you in to see the stone 50m inside the park. Take time out to enjoy the views to north and west from the front of the café. If it's raining console a wallaby.

4. THE ROMAN STONE.
This stone stands by the B827 400m south of Comrie. There is no suitable parking by the stone. Coming from anywhere in Comrie walk south to the end of Dalginross (the 1km tree lined 'boulevard' that runs straight from the main square). At the crossroads, where the main road turns right to leave the village 200m beyond, go straight head up the small residential road. After about 400m take the farm track on your right which meets, after another 400m, the B827 by the stone. Carry on straight beyond the stone for 100m then first right first left and 600m beyond you will be by the Tumuli or Burial Cairns by the Water of Ruchill mentioned with BALMUICK. The aerial

©CROWN COPYRIGHT:RCAHMS

picture shows the ghostly Roman remains with, on the right, the 'marching' Camp of 23 acres for a temporary garrison of around 4000 men perhaps engaged to build, on the left, the Fort of perhaps 4 acres for a more permanent garrison of around 1000.

This was one of the series of around 10 'glenblocking' forts ranged up the highland boundary fault line from the Clyde to Strathcarrow near the East coast at Brechin. According to the Roman geographer Strabo this north west Frontier was, *"The last, loneliest and loveliest outpost of the Roman Empire"...which.. "at it's greatest ran from the Ethiopian Circle in the South to the Earn in the North."*

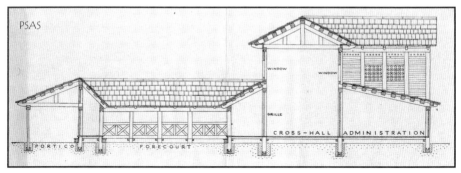

A cross section through one of the buildings of the Romans camp at Fendoch (at the mouth of the Sma Glen) gives an idea of the nature of their buildings.

5.DUNMOID

This site lies some 800m north west of the Roman Stone. From the south end of Dalginross head west out of the village on the Crieff back road. 300m from the cross-roads, in an edge clearing in the woods by the road, this little roundel sits by the wall of the village graveyard. In winter the Ben Halton range lies clear between the tree trunks to the west. In summer the place is a dense leafy glade open to the north.

6.CRAGGISH

Although no stones remain here the walk is pleasant and easy and you are soon delivered into an amphitheatre of hills and mountains. Follow the main road (A85 out of Comrie west towards St Fillans) . A few hundred metres before the west end of the village take a left across the elegant Ross Bridge of 1792. 300m from the bridge you will pass the Earthquake House perched atop the fault line and originally home for one of the worlds very earliest seismographs. Walk this road for about 1km and follow round the sharp left bend at Craggish Farm. The stones lay off to the left (east) side of the road in an uncultivated strip 400m from the corner. If hot walk on a further 1km and take a dip at Comrie's favourite swimming hole 'The Lynn'. Note the White Church in the distance its clock face blank towards the Ross whose residents 2 centuries past declined to contribute to its costs. Present residents are generally charitable and kind.

7.TOM na CHESSAIG

Walk to the great heaven bound sandstone space rocket on its launch pad that is the Church of Scotland on Burrell Street at the west end of the village. Facing the church front wander up the right (west) side and you will come to the river Earn in about 70m. The scrubby little hummock is where the stone circle sat. Comrie is replete with eateries from where you can study booklets of the many delightful walks around, few more exciting than round the heaped aisles of the Cancer Charity Shop with an old graveyard hard by to wander through centuries in minutes by the swift flowing river Earn.

8.L AWERS

This stone stands in a field generally graced by fine horses whose owners, gazing down from the Adam windows of the great house, would rightly be most vexed to see amateur antiquarians galumphing amongst the thoroughbreds. Park at one of the lay-bys 2kms east of Comrie and, taking great care on this busy trunk road, navigate the verge towards the corner at the lodge entrance to Lawers House. The stone can be seen around 120m into the field to the south of the road.

9. CLATHICK.

This stone is a challenge to see. It is 600m north of the A85 up the steep burn which crosses the road by Carse of Trowan Farm road end 3.5km east of Comrie. There is no suitable parking around here and the road is fast and bendy. One option might be to park at the lay by 2km east of Comrie and walk the road verge a perilous 800m east then take a left up the old quarry track past Ballaig. After about 800 m of a steep climb the track appears through Home Wood. Leave the track to the right and follow the edge of the wood 200m east then 300m as it turns down hill to the south east. The stones are on a little promontory all a-tumble of small stones down to a bend in the burn. Note that the metamorphic swirl of the stone layers at the top of the stone seems to echo the twist and swirl of the steep burn as it encounters this place. Another option for the Clathick stone might be to walk in from the farm tracks that lead over from Glen Turret 3km east but the 1:25000 Crieff NN 82/92 O.S. map would be required company along with sufficient nouse to sensibly navigate a shooting estate. It is a modest stone and those less enthusiastic about the *genius loci* of the Neolithic might be underwhelmed by oe'r strenuous and perilous a route march.

If by the A85 in the vicinity of this stone regardless of mode of transport take the road 0.7km East of Carse of Trowan farm road end which links with the Comrie Crieff back road. After 0.5km take a right and walk the old railway line back Comrie. This is pretty overgrown at points. Alternatively carry on to the back road and take it west back into Comrie passing, after 400m, a Neolithic tree clad cairn at Strowan.

10. BALMUICK

There are no such impediments to the enjoyment of this place lying as it does on open heather moorland by a much wandered hill track. Get dropped of by the bus at Fordie Farm Road end 2km east of Comrie or park in one of the aforementioned lay byes 100m east. Walk straight up the farm track past Lawers Farm following the burn up

74

through the woods for 1km. The track veers west, crosses the burn and after skirting the woods for 800m heads north. Going straight through any apparent cross tracks after 2km or so the stones should be seen on a steep hummock 200m north of a sharp right bend in the track. There are cairns on the hillock 800m west and an ancient hut and field system noted 500m north west. You'll probably walk 10 km there and back climbing 300m in the process so, sturdy heart and replete sandwich pouch would greatly help. So too a pair of binoculars for this place, the highest of the Stones of Strathearn, provides the perfect backdrop for imagining Eagledom.

11. TULLYBANNOCHER

The St Fillans bus may be able to drop you off at the farm road end on the long straight away 1.5km west of Comrie. Alternatively park at the Tullybannocher Café, go have a coffee and sticky bun, then cross the road and enter the field to the left (west) of the little white cottage opposite the Café. This field is often waterlogged in parts or filled with crop or beast so skirt around the edge beside the road. After about 500m follow the burn perpendicular to the road (north). As you walk up the burn the stones will be visible 200m away on your left. After about 500m you will come to farm gates and a place to safely cross the burn from where you can double back into the standing stone field. Aberuchill Castle can be seen to the south at the foot of Ben Halton. On a platform above the Earn in 20/- Wood and only about 800m east of the stones this 6 ton flat top stone was perhaps levelled in ancient times with the chocking stone seen below the short edge.

12. DRUIM na CILLE

Once you have visited TULLYBANNOCHER head north up the farm track into the hills. After about 500m, at a dishevelled tractor shed, follow the track left. Some of the earth works you encounter to left and right may be reminiscent of the work of the ancients but is in fact the doings of the Royal & Ancients...a proposed golf course which started then fizzled out some years ago. After about 1km this gently rising track joins the Maam Road the ancient principle thoroughfare west when once the lower ground was undrained wetland. Take the Maam road left (west) though remember this junction as it opens up the opportunity later of going right (east) and under the quartz outcrop to appear out at the Lednock Road from where you can walk back to Comrie or strike a path over the shakey bridge and up the east side of the Lednock to visit BALMUICK. After about 500m west the road forks left, down into Dunira Estate, or right up the hill. Follow the track about 800m uphill and you will come to the site with the stones laying in a sorry row parallel to the road with the cup marked stone early in the line. Take the path towards the phone mast and the cairn circle is some 50m in on the right hand side. It is well worth walking up the Maam Road a further 1km at least till it rounds the bend to follow the gorge of the Boltican

It also leads in time to St Fillans where many wonders can be visited before taking the bus back to base. There are cup marked rocks on the hillside north west of St Fillans, and a fairy rock or two within its boundaries. 1 km east sits the intriguing little rocky hill called Dundurn , associated with Saint Fillan and first noted in history by one of St Columba's scribes as a Pictish Citadel at the western end of the Pictish province of Strathearn. An ancient cairn attends east of Dundurn at Kindrochet.

1.AIRTHEY   STONES of the OCHILL FRINGE

On the eastern edge of Bridge of Allan you will come to the main road entrance of the Stirling University campus. Beguile the sentries with the passion of your pilgrimage and enter the campus. Turn left before the 'loch' and follow the road round to Airthey Castle and the playing fields. En route you will spot the towering peculiarity of a stone lurking by the road edge in the woods. Park by the University golf course and make your way across to the rugby fields where the great megalith stands. Take a stroll to the southern edge of the plateau to gaze out across the Devon basin and the impressive southern escarpments of the Ochills.

2.GLENHEAD

Leave the A9 at junction 11 taking the B824 for Doune. In about 3kms park on the north side of the road at the visitor car park for the memorial to David Sutherland ,the

DUNBLANE

founder of the SAS ,who stands there on his plinth bronze great coat a-flap. The stones lie 200m from the main road 100m to the north of the farm track to Glenhead. This field is in regular crop so access might be restricted. Maybe best to walk the main road verge 150m east then follow the fence line up to the stones. Even if the field seems simply grassed this may be for silage and tramping it foolhardy.

Return to the track and head north towards Glenhead. After 500m the track veers left and 200m beyond, just before the private house on your left, a short overgrown wooded track leads off to the right. Within 100m you will come to a field. Staying on the wooded side walk the edge of the field north for a few metres and the great slab stands by the fence line. Go doon t Doune for a wander then visit Dunblane Cathedral before exploring further .

3.CUPARLAW

Come up onto Sheriffmuir from Dunblane, Bridge of Allan (spectacular views down the Forth) or up from Blackford and park at the Sheriffmuir Inn and refresh yourself before walking south down the minor road that heads to Bridge of Allan. After about 2.5km the road rounds a wood on the right and a small farm shed sits on the west side of the road. Follow the farm track up past the shed heading north west and in about 200m strike a line for the highpoint to your left (south west). Mounting the crest the view is breathtaking far down the Forth, back over the Wallace monument & Stirling and south east through the gap in the mountain eminences to the Pentlands behind Edinburgh.

The Sheriffmuir Inn is about 3km East of Dunblane. If stopping at the Inn the 'Wallace Stone' can just be seem 600m east in the field opposite. If you are coming up from Dunblane take a left at the T junction and pass the Inn. The road swings right and climbs the hill. In about 600m you come to a lay-by on the left. From here cross into the field and walking due south (from the lay-by diagonally to the right) you will come upon the stones in about 200m. Here was the site of the bloody Battle of Sheriffmuir in 1715 where superior numbers of Jacobites were defeated by government forces the Old Pretender having slept in or such so missing the action.

5. WHITE STONE

This stone is awkward to get to but you can stop off at the lay-by on the south bound M9 10km south west of Blackford (1km after the Balhaldie filling station) and take the view. The stone lies 250m off in the field.

6. WESTER BIGGS

About 6 km north west of the Sheriffmuir Inn, just beyond a great telecoms mast, pause and savour the qualities of a place once adorned with a stone circle.

7. THE BOAT STONE

About 1.5km beyond Wester Biggs past a wood on the left then one on the right the road begins to fall towards Blackford 2km ahead. Up near the tree line of the woods on the left (west) , some 30m from the road, the stone lies fallen in a field.

8. GLENEAGLES

If you have driven over Sheriffmuir rejoin the A9 at Blackford and leave it 5km later at the Gleneagles/Crieff junction. Take a right onto the A823 and head south east over the motorway . Immediately over the bridge turn right onto a section of the old A9 now an access road serving a number of farms up in the mouth of Glen Eagles. If arriving by car leave it parked sensibly up by the gate. 100m down this road you will see stone (A) 20m off in the field to the left (south) and stone (B) 300m further west in the lower field 50m off the road as it bends south.

9. EASTHILL

There are many ways to get to this stone so I suggest only the most basic assuming you have just visited Gleneagles stones. Take the B823 Crieff road north and 500m beyond the main entrance to Gleneagles Hotel take a right at the mini roundabout cross roads. After 500m take a left at the next mini roundabout and the stones appear at a road junction 500m beyond. This may look a quiet little country junction but it is often a-throb with tractors and buses. There is no suitable parking close by so best find a safe parking space in the nearby residential area and walk to the site. 2km north east of these stones the delightfully sited and remarkable 15th century Tullibardine Chapel should engage the weariest soul.

Leave Auchterarder on the old main road (A9) heading north east and in about 6km note the road junction across from St Cattan's - the medieval chapel above a bend in the Ruthven Water. Park wisely in the village and walk back to this junction. Take a right on the minor road to Kinkell Bridge and turn immediately right up the farm track to Belhie. This is private farmed land so you must be conscientious in your country code. After about 1km, at a bend in an otherwise straight section of track, follow the farm track to right. After about 300m you should see the stone 300m north east in the middle of the left hand field. This field is regularly in crop or grazed so access to the stone may not be appropriate though skirting the wooded edge opens up great vistas around the compass.

Leave Aberuthven heading north east up the A9 to Perth . In about 2km take the B9141 for 3km to Dunning. Park or tether safely in Dunning and pause to appreciate the 800 year old tower of St Serf's (who is reputed to have built a small chapel here in the 5th century). Visit the church and be overwhelmingly charmed by the Dupplin Cross Perthshire's most spectacular Pictish monument from the 9th Century. From the main square walk north down Kirk Wynd beside the church till it joins the Dunning Burn. Follow for 100 m more then

take the lane off to the left which leads to a field in 50m. The stone lies 50m off in the field.

There is no suitable place to park so reconnoitre for a nearish lay-by or walk out from Dunning on the Yetts o'Muckhart road south (B934). After a 3 km hike and a rise of some 200m, just past the entrance road to Knowes Farm, the farm owners have kindly installed a wee gate with sign for the Grey Stone. Climb up and carefully cross the field and after about 300m you should spot the stone in a field some 300m north east (to the right) of the farm. Again this is a private farm and all the fields tend to be grazed so great care needs to be exercised though if you encounter the owners, and you are not being wantonly stupid, you will likely find a warm and enthusiastic welcome.

1 km out on the road west from the main square you will come upon this plaintive little cross dedicated to the last witch burnt around these parts. These days we are generally kinder to witches.

Walking with Stones

In 2009 in the wonderful Autumn walking festival based in Crieff that is the Drovers' Tryst I lead a walk titled 'Walking with Stones' which attempted to thread together some of the Standing Stones sites around the town. On the opposite page I reprint the 'walk brochure'. The walking party left Crieff on the bus around 9.30am and walked the route shown in black at an easy pace returning to the town around 4pm. The route is served with a decent track or roadway most of the way barring the fields around CROFTHEAD and from FOULFORD till it crosses the A822. The walk is around 17km (11 miles) and rises over 250m (900ft)

Take the early morning bus out of Crieff and get off at the Fowlis Wester crossroads. The tree clad mound hereby is a Neolithic cairn with what might be called a standing stone on its flank. 500m further up this road you will see a standing stone on the left in front of the house named Shannacher. This was recently erected by the owners following its chance discovery under the garden during works to install geo thermal heating pipework. Walk up into Fowlis Wester, visit the delightful Kirk, contribute to the collection box, then follow the track west (formerly the main road) out of the village. Visit **CROFTHEAD** stones (see pgs 25+ 67).

Leave the stones head north west follow the burn up the hill and, beyond the grazing fields, strike east uphill across the heather moor till you spot the **MOOR of ARDOCH** stones. If the fields are unsuitable go back to the village and walk the road north (see pgs 23+67). Leave the stones and follow the track west, down past Loch Meallbrodden, then up to a saddle in the Bracketriggs Hills. With a track heading left to Milquanzie Hill head right up to see the cup marked rock, the 'fallen stone' and spectacular views from the summit. (pg 68). Weather permitting a fine lunch spot. Reflect on the time, effort and money being put into conservation measures on this land by Abercairney Estates and ensure your dog stays on the leash. Nesting bird colonies will give up on an area if frequently dog bothered.

Return to the main track and head down to **FOULFORD** (pg 30+68). If open enjoy the Inn. Around the back of the Inn and up towards the house there is a gate in the fence heading west. Navigating the contour across these fields will vary dependant on crop and livestock. If in doubt walk the main road south west. Traffic can be fast on this road so great care is needed. Either way, around 1km south west of the Inn, you will come to a farm track which leaves the main road and runs a delightful Fault Line path down into Monzie. Visit the church then walk the road 1km south east to visit **MONZIE** stones (pg 27). An alternative route, walking down the Monzie Joinery entrance drive then keeping left via Monzie Castle estate roads, may be possible if livestock and open gates permit. Remember the Castle is a private house so don't wander nearby. Leave the stones and walk round The Knock (details pg 68) to **FERNTOWER** (pg 29+68) from where you can wander down into Crieff for much needed sustenance.

I have only once navigated the 'alternative route' via **STONFIELD** and my path was fraught with bogs, burns, deer fences, livestock and the frisson necessarily emitting from a working shooting estate so great care, consideration and time needed.

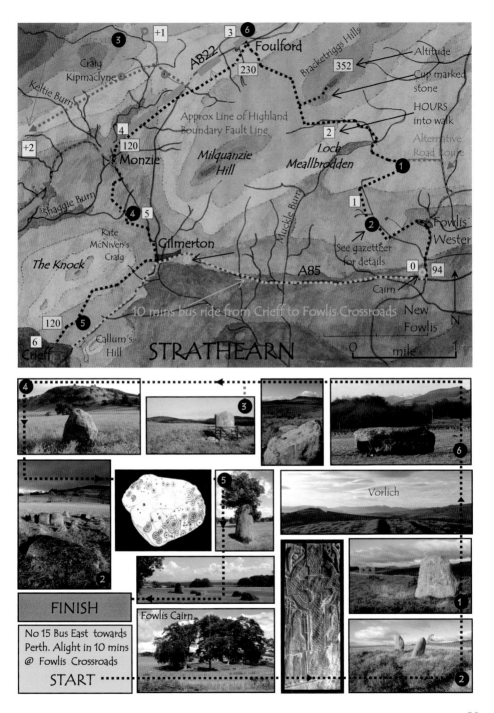

+1

3

3

6

Foulford

A822

230

Bracketriggs Hills

352

Altitude

Cup marked stone

HOURS into walk

Craig Kipmaclyne

Keltie Burn

Approx Line of Highland Boundary Fault Line

Milquanzie Hill

Loch Meallbrodden

Alternative Road Route

4

120

+2

Monzie

Shaggie Burn

4

5

Kate McNiven's Craig

The Knock

Gilmerton

Muckle Burn

2

1

2

See gazetteer for details

1

Fowlis Wester

0

94

A85

Cairn

10 mins bus ride from Crieff to Fowlis Crossroads

New Fowlis

N

120

5

6

Crieff

Callum's Hill

STRATHEARN

0   mile   1

4

3

6

Vorlich

5

2

1

FINISH

No 15 Bus East towards Perth. Alight in 10 mins @ Fowlis Crossroads

START

Fowlis Cairn

2

80

Walking in to the Future

Two more day trip walking possibilities worthy of exploration are;
GLENEAGLES TO COMRIE—along the Coire Odhar
From a train decant at Gleneagles station I can imagine walking from the great rent in the Ochills that is **GLENEAGLES** and its attendant stones, past **EASTHILL** stones, Tullibardine Chapel and on to the **DALCHIRLA** alignment. A quiet country road walk would then take you to **DUNRUCHAN** and its complex delights from where you could skirt round Beinn Dubh and through to **AUCHINGARRICH** then down over the hill track to the **ROMAN STONE** and thence to **DUMOID** before repairing to a Comrie tavern to bathe your 30km trodden feet.
MUTHILL TO COMRIE
A less taxing version of around 18km might deliver you to Muthill by bus for a wander around its old kirk and tea room before heading out on the country roads to **DALCHIRLA** then, as above, to Comrie.

The directions above are vague as I have done neither walk but reckon, equipped with OS Explorer map 368 and a healthy respect for Countryside Codes, fine day outs could be had. I hope this book may prove a catalyst to the exploration of other walking and cycling routes that weave together connections between the stones but again I cannot stress enough how important it is that anyone visiting these places, particularly on the strength of this book, should show an unimpeachable respect for the countryside and the folk who live and work in it.

These stones have stood here for some 4000 years and are likely to be still standing 4000 years from now when much of our present human endeavour has turned to dust. The common denominator of our basic humanity however threads relentlessly through the aeons and so we can yet lie by a stone, in the sun, heady with the scent of sweet grasses, beguiled by the plaintive call of the curlew, sleep and dream of timeless things. I hope this book encourages you to do just that.

Note– no crops were damaged in either the taking of this photograph or the dreaming of that dream..

Notes

1	Blood of the Isles	Sykes,B.C 2006 Bantam
2	Neolithic & Bronze Age Scotland	Ashmore,P.J 2005 pg19
3	Kilmartin. Introduction & Guide	Butler, Rachel 1999 p55
	Stone Circles of Britain Ireland & Brittany	Burl,A 2000 pg29
4	Britain 3000BC	Castelton,R 2003 pg3
5	Kilmartin. Introduction & Guide	Butler, Rachel 1999 p5
6	Britain 3000BC	Castelton,R 2003 pg3
7	The Perthshire Book	Omand,D 1999 pg20
8	First Settlers in Crammond, Edinburgh, 8500BC	Scotsman 26&30.5.01
9	Britain 3000BC	Castelton,R 2003 pg6
10	The Perthshire Book	Omand,D 1999 pg21
11	Stone Circles of Britain Ireland & Brittany	Burl,A 2000 pg5
12	A Short History of Myth	Armstrong, K 2005
13	The Perthshire Book	Omand,D 1999 pg24
14	PSAS vol 107 1976	Ritchie,J.N.G 1976
15	Stone Circles of Britain Ireland & Brittany	Burl,A 2000 pg249
16	Neolithic & Bronze Age Scotland	Ashmore,P.J 2005 pg70
17	The Perthshire Book	Omand,D 1999 pg26
18	PSAS Vol 68 Feb12 1934	Mitchell.M.E.C
19	Bronze Age Britain	Pearson,M.P 2005
20	Stone Circles of Britain Ireland & Brittany	Burl,A 2000 pg393
21	Stone Circles of Britain Ireland & Brittany	Burl,A 2000 pg3
22	Stone Circles of Britain Ireland & Brittany	Burl,A 2000 pg66
23	Stone Circles of Britain Ireland & Brittany	Burl,A 2000 pg75
24	The Modern Antiquarian	Cope,J. pg68
25	The Sun, Moon & Standing Stones	Wood,J.E. 1978
26	PSAS Vol 68 Jan 8th 1934	Kilbride-Jones,H.E.
27	Stone Circles of Britain Ireland & Brittany	Burl,A 2000 pg41
28	The Campus, The Cursus and The Stayt	Mayall,C

More confession than note it has to be said that whilst this book boasts of gazetteering all the stones in an area it is inevitably a fleeting conceit. Just a few weeks before going to print I was directed to a standing stone quite off my radar yet under my nose in Crieff. There will be others and maybe future technologies and deepening awareness will show this study to have been just the tip of a stoneberg.

And to those enraged by my mixing of metres, feet and inches forgive me but its just the way some of us find useful in contemplating a multiverse indifferent to standardisation.

Acknowledgements

Thanks for encouragement and advice to; Noel Fojut, Ann McSween & Allan Duffy of Historic Scotland, Erin Osborne-Martin of the Society of Antiquaries, Eila MacQueen of Archaeology Scotland, David Strachan of Perth & Kinross Heritage Trust, Tertia Barnett of RCAHMS, Mark Hall at Perth Museum, Paul McLennan of Perth & Kinross Countryside Trust, Councillor Ann Cowan of Perth & Kinross Council, local historians & authors Colin Mayall & David Cowan, Bill Armit (who knows a bag of spanners when he sees it) and my enthusiastic friends; Fin, Giles, Peter, Caroline, Angie, Neil, Helena, Julie, two Johns, Keith, and Sabrina. Special thanks to my ever present and uncomplaining companion Oscar and to my patient family. Inspiration from and greatest respect to Julian Cope and Aubrey Burl.

Without access to the land this project would not have been possible so I am indebted to the owners and tenants of the land who graciously suffered my intrusions.

I am grateful to the Society of Antiquaries of Scotland for permission to reproduce the many illustrations from their Proceedings noted PSAS in the text and below.

In 1910 Fred R Coles published, in the Proceedings of the Society 'A Report on stone circles in Perthshire, principally Strathearn' which, to my understanding, is the only previous attempt to gazetteer the stones of this area and proved a great source of information and inspiration. Many thanks to the contributors of the other illustrations noted below.

pg	ILLUSTRATION	SOURCE
8	Balls of Scotland	Ludovic MacLellan Mann 1913, PSAS 12 pg 410
10	Jet Beads	National Museum of Scotland
10	Jadeite Axehead	University of Aberdeen, Jadeite Axehead, from Methlick, Aberdeenshire,
10	Beaker pot	M.E.Crichton Mitchell 1935, PSAS 69, pg 398
12	Quartz Tools	Alison Young 1943, PSAS 77, pg 181
14	Callanish	inspired by drawing in Julian Cope's Modern Antiquarian
19	Satelitte Photo	NASA
24	Quartz tools	Alison Young 1943, PSAS 77, pg 181
31	Clach Ossian plan	Fred R Coles 1910, PSAS 45,pg 94
32	Clach na Tiompan plan	Fred R Coles 1910, PSAS 45,pg 100
36	Duchlage sketch	Fred R Coles 1910, PSAS 45,pg 76
38	Dalchirla sketch	Fred R Coles 1910, PSAS 45,pg71
39	Dunruchan plan	Fred R Coles 1910, PSAS 45,pg 67
41	Cup & Ring photos	George Currie
42	Roman Stone plans	Fred R Coles 1910, PSAS 45,pg 59
43	Dunmoid plan	Fred R Coles 1910, PSAS 45,pg 57
46	Balmuick plan	Fred R Coles 1910, PSAS 45,pg 52
48	Druim na Cille plan	Fred R Coles 1910, PSAS 45,pg 48
69	Foulford sketch	David Cowan
71	Drummond Castle photo	Nick Haynes
72	Roman Camp ariel photo	Crown Copyright:RCAHMS. Licensor www.rcahms.gov.uk
73	Fendoch sketch	Richmond & McIntyre 1939, PSAS 73, pg 126

Bibliography

GOOD,GENERAL, WELL ILLUSTRATED HISTORIES OF THE PERIOD	
ASHMORE, Patrick J	**Neolithic & Bronze Age Scotland**
	1996-Batsford/Historic Scotland-128pgs
PEARSON, Michael P	**Bronze Age Britain**
	2005-Batsford/Engish Heritage- 144pgs
CASTLEDEN,Rodney	**Britain 3000 BC**
	2003-Sutton-212pgs.
RITCHIE, Anna	**Scotland BC**
	1994- HMSO Edinburgh/Historic Scotland-80pgs
MORE RICHLY DETAILED EXPLORATIONS OF THE SUBJECT	
BURL, Aubrey	**The Stone Circles of Britain,Ireland & Brittany**
	2000-Yale University Press- 461pgs
PITTS,Mike	**Hengeworld**
	2001-Arrow Books-409pgs
PRYOR, Francis	**Britain BC**
	2004-Harper Perennial-488pgs
WOOD, John Edwin	**The Sun,Moon & Standing Stones**
	1978-Oxford University Press
BURL, Aubrey	Last 4 decades- Any Publication-Countless pgs
BUTLER,Racfhel	**Kilmartin. An Introduction & Guide**
	1999- Kilmartin House Trust
EXUBERANT, EVOCATIVE, LAVISHLY ILLUSTRATED WORKS OF LOVE	
COPE, Julian	**The Modern Antiquarian**
	1998-Thorsons-438pgs
COPE, Julian	**The Megalithic European**
	2004-Harper Collins-496pgs
INTRODUCTIONS TO THE CONTEXT OF BELIEF	
LEWIS-WILLIAMS,David	**Inside the Neolithic Mind**
& PEARCE, David	2005-Thames&Hudson-320pgs
ARMSTRONG,Karen	**A Short History of Myth**
	2005-Canongate Books Ltd-159pgs
PROCEEDINGS OF THE SOCIETY OF SCOTTISH ANTIQUARIES	
These are the publications I consulted for much of the detail on individual sites:	
YOUNG,Alison	**Circle of stones Monzie castle**
& MITCHELL,Margaret C	1882- PSSA 16 Feb 13 1882-6pgs
BOSTON,Thomas	**Notes on 3 sepulchral mounds Balmuick , Comrie**
	1884-PSSA 18 Apr 14 1884-3pgs
COLES,Fred R	**Report on stone circles in Perthshire. Principally Strathearn**
	1910-PSSA 45 Dec 12 1910-56pgs
YOUNG,Alison	**Report on excavation at Monzie**
& MITCHELL,Margaret C	1939-PSSA 73-Jan 9 1939-11pgs
YOUNG,Alison	**Report on Standing Stones & other remains, Fowlis Wester**
	1943-PSSA 77-read Oct 16 1943-11pgs

LOCAL GUIDES	
OMAND,Donald	**The Perthshire Book**
	1999-Birlinn Ltd-255pgs
HAYNES, Nick	**Perth & Kinross an illustrated architectural guide**
	2000-Rutloand Press-240pgs
P&K HERITAGE TRUST	**A Cycle of Saints**-The Medieval Chapels of Strathearn
	The Romans in Perthshire
MAYALL, Colin	**The Campus, The Cursus and the Stayt**
	Available Crieff Library (& check his many other titles in the shops)
COWAN, David &	**Ley Lines and Earth Energies**
ARNOLD,Chris	Counter Culture Books (available from www.leyman.demon.co.uk)

ASSORTED WEBSITES
www.onetreeislandpublishing.com
A modest site to promote this book.
www.themodernantiquarian.com
Julian Cope's continued, wonderful and encyclopaedic contribution to everything megalithic.
www.droverstryst.com
Details of Strathearn's annual autumn walking festival.
rockartuk.fotopic.net
Database central for all things petroglyphic
www.pkht.org.uk
Perth&Kinross Heritage Trust- Database of all things archaeological in the county.
www.pkct.org.uk
Perth & Kinross Countryside Trust-Access codes, other walks and cycling info.
www.leyman.demon.co.uk
David Cowan's introduction to Earth Energies as witnessed around Strathearn and beyond.
..and doing just what they say on the tin...
www.stagecoach.com/timetables
www.crieffandstrathearn.co.uk
www.perthshire-scotland.co.uk
www.comrie.org.uk
www.dunblaneweb.co.uk
www.dunning.uk.net
www.finlaysonarchitects.co.uk

Andrew Finlayson just happens to be an architect fortunate enough to live and work in Strathearn who, with the advent of the digital camera, stumbled upon a rich seam of ancient place making whose genius loci was so potent as to incite the making of this tribute .